This is
Citizenship 2

Julia Fiehn Terry Fiehn

Although every effort has been made to ensure that website addresses are correct at time of going to press, Hodder Education cannot be held responsible for the content of any website mentioned in this book. It is sometimes possible to find a relocated web page by typing in the address of the home page for a website in the URL window of your browser.

Hachette UK's policy is to use papers that are natural, renewable and recyclable products and made from wood grown in sustainable forests. The logging and manufacturing processes are expected to conform to the environmental regulations of the country of origin.

Orders: please contact Bookpoint Ltd, 130 Milton Park, Abingdon, Oxon OX14 4SB. Telephone: (44) 01235 827720. Fax: (44) 01235 400454. Lines are open 9.00–5.00, Monday to Saturday, with a 24-hour message answering service. Visit our website at www.hoddereducation.co.uk

Cover photo: © Gary Jochim/Superstock
Illustrations by Karen Donelly, Richard Duszczak, Peter Greenwood, Tony Jones, Janek Matysiak, Oxford Designers and Illustrators, Tony Randell, Chris Rothero, Steve Smith
Designed in 11/14pt Frutiger by Stephen Rowling/Springworks
Printed in Italy

A catalogue record for this title is available from the British Library

ISBN: 978 0340 947 128

Titles in the series

This is Citizenship 1 Pupil's Book 978 0340 947 098
This is Citizenship 1 Teacher's Resource 978 0340 947 104
This is Citizenship 1 Dynamic Learning 978 0340 947 111

This is Citizenship 2 Pupil's Book 978 0340 947 128
This is Citizenship 2 Teacher's Resource 978 0340 947 135
This is Citizenship 2 Dynamic Learning 978 0340 947 142

This is Citizenship 3 Pupil's Book 978 0340 947 159
This is Citizenship 3 Teacher's Resource 978 0340 947 166
This is Citizenship 3 Dynamic Learning 978 0340 947 173

Contents

The Publishers would like to thank the following for permission to reproduce copyright material:

Photo credits
p.4 © Jonathan Player/Rex Features; **p.10** *All Photos* With kind permission of Headliners (UK), www.headliners.org; **p.26** *t* © Barry Batchelor/PA Photos, *c* © Jeff Morgan social issues/Alamy, *b* © Janine Wiedel Photolibrary/Alamy; **p.27** © PA Archive/PA Photos **p.54** with permission from Maqsood Ahmad; **p.56** © Show Racism the Red Card/ www.theredcard.org, used with permission; **p.66** *l* © Shakil Pathan/Anti-Slavery International, *r* © CHRD/ Handout/epa/Corbis; **p.67** *t* © Ricardo Funari /BrazilPhotos/Alamy, *b* © Sadarnando Mondol/with kind permission of the Church Mission Society; **p.68** © Grace Kassab/AP/PA Photos; **pp.70–71** © Janine Wiedel Photolibrary/Alamy; **p.73** © ITV / Rex Features; **p.74** *tr* © Matt Cardy/Alamy, *bl* © Malcolm Case-Green/Alamy; **p.76** *t* © Stefano Rellandini/Reuters/Corbis, *b* © Jon Hrusa/epa/Corbis; **p.77** Illustration from 'One Day We Had to Run!: Refugee Children tell Their Stories in Words and Paintings', Sybella Wilkes (Evans Brothers Limited, London). Courtesy of UNHCR. Used with permission; **p.78** © Markus Matzel/Das Fotoarchiv./Still Pictures; **p.79** *tl* © Ton Koene/Still Pictures, *tr* © Alison Wright/CORBIS, *b* © Jane Mingay/Rex Features; **p.86, 88** with kind permission of Amnesty International.

Acknowledgements
p.8–9, Nacro, quotes from *Wasted Lives*, reproduced by kind permission of Nacro; **p.10–11**, Headliners, 'Gangs: What's the attraction?' © Headliners. Headliners is a news agency and learning through journalism programme run for and by young people aged 8–19. www.headliners.org; **p.44**, Wandsworth Borough Council, projected expenditure on Council services, 2008/9 (reproduced on a pie chart); **p.56–57**, Elliot Joseph, 'Goal' from *Pitchprose.org website* (2004); **p.66, 67**, Anti-Slavery International, extracts on bonded labour and forced labour from *www.antislavery.org*, reproduced by permission of the publisher; **p.67**, Church Mission Society, case study on Sabina (adapted), reproduced by permission of the Church Mission Society; **p.73**, Central Independent Television, extract from *Auf Wiedersehen, Pet,* DVD: Episode 1 – 'If I Were a Carpenter' (1983); **p.74**, Neil Mackay, article, 'The New Scots: Immigrants' Stories' (adapted) from *The Sunday Herald* (August 27, 2006), reproduced by permission of the author; **p.76–77, 78** *t*, UNHCR, extracts (adapted) from *Refugee Children*, reproduced by permission of UNHCR; **p.78** *b*, LSN/QIA, 'Teshk's Story' from *We All Came Here from Somewhere – diversity, identities and citizenship, www.post16citizenship.org* (LSN/QIA, 2006), reproduced by permission of Quality Improvement Agency; **p.79** extracts from *Starting over: young refugees talk about life in Britain* (The Prince's Trust/The Diana, Princess of Wales Memorial Fund, 2002), reproduced by permission of The Diana, Princess of Wales Memorial Fund; **p.86**, Amnesty International UK, extracts (adapted) from Amnesty International website.

Section 1

Rules and fairness, rights and responsibilities

How does the law affect young people?

What are Youth Offending Teams and how do they work?

What are the consequences of crime?

Why do young people commit crimes?

What happens in Youth Courts?

All groups of people need rules to protect their rights and ensure that people can get on together. Rules become laws when they are given the backing of the government of the country. Laws are written down and are enforced by the police. When people are accused of breaking the law, they are taken to court to try to find out if they are guilty or innocent. Courts can punish people found guilty of committing crimes. People sometimes disagree about how fair laws are, and about the way they are enforced. Crime has consequences for the offenders, the victims and society at large.

KEY WORDS

court

justice

law

legal system

magistrate

offender

sentence

Assessing your progress
In this section you will be assessing how well you can:

• give your opinion and explain it to others
• listen to and take other people's opinions into account
• make a case for a point of view
• make decisions
• decide what you think is fair
• understand issues to do with youth crime and justice.

1

1.1 How does the law affect young people?

The law should treat all adults the same. It is an important part of the legal system of the UK that the same laws apply to everyone. But the law allows young people to do different things at different ages. How much do you know about your legal rights and duties?

Activity

1 Work in pairs. At what age do you think you can do the things shown on pages 2–3? See how many you can get right. Your teacher will tell you the correct answers at the end.
2 Why are you allowed to do different things at different ages?
3 Which of these laws do you think are unfair?
4 Choose just one and plan an argument explaining why you would like to see the law changed to a different age. Give at least two reasons and explain them well.

1 Be held to be criminally responsible

2 Buy a pet

3 Get a part-time job

4 Go into a pub

5 Get a custodial sentence for a crime

6 See a 15 certificate film

12 Marry with parent's consent

11 Give consent to heterosexual and homosexual activity

10 Fly an aeroplane

9 Buy fireworks

8 Buy alcohol

7 Leave school and get a full-time job

13 Buy cigarettes and tobacco

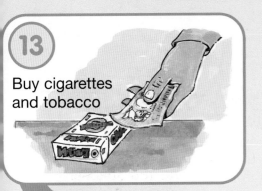

27 Gamble (place a bet)

26 Be entitled to the National Minimum Wage (full adult rate)

14 Join the armed forces

25 Adopt a child

15 Play the National Lottery

24 Stand for Parliament

16 Drive a car and motorcycle

23 Be entitled to the National Minimum Wage (young person's rate)

22 Leave home without your parents' consent

17 Have a tattoo

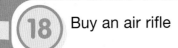

21 Buy a house

18 Buy an air rifle

19 Vote

20 Sign a tenancy agreement

How are young people affected by measures to stop anti-social behaviour?

The behaviour of some young people, particularly groups of young people in public places, worries some adults. Older people sometimes feel intimidated by large groups of youths or they complain about their noise and rowdiness – their anti-social behaviour. This is legally defined as behaviour that 'unduly disturbs, harasses or alarms the public and the community as a whole'.

Various attempts have been made to stop this behaviour. Here are some.

ASBOs

Anti-Social Behaviour Orders (ASBOs) are designed to stop the behaviour that spoils the quality of life for people in a neighbourhood. The police or the local council can ask the courts to make an order against someone. They are often applied to young people but they can be given to anyone of any age. People in the community can collect evidence against someone's anti-social habits, such as a noisy gathering, vandalism or general nuisance. ASBOs last for two years. If a person does not obey the ASBO they can be given more serious punishments, even going to prison.

Dispersal of groups

The police can be given powers to disperse people in public places, like shopping arcades or town centres, where groups gather to intimidate or harass the public. They can stop groups of two or more people from entering the area for up to 24 hours if the police feel they are behaving in an anti-social way. They can also drive home under-sixteens if they are found on the streets after 9p.m.

The Mosquito

This is a device that sends out a high ultra-sonic tone that is very unpleasant to the ears of young people and makes them move away from the areas quickly. The majority of people over 25 are unable to hear this ultra-sonic frequency.

Activity

Work in pairs or threes.

1 Read the statements on page 5. Which do you agree with and which do you disagree with?

2 When you've read them, decide what your opinions are about the three methods of controlling anti-social behaviour. Be prepared to explain your views to the rest of the class.

A Some young people take no notice of ASBOs and just continue the same behaviour.

B It is young people who are often the victims of anti-social behaviour, so ASBOs help protect them as well as older people.

C They can stop gang members meeting in particular places and from seeing each other if they have ASBOs at the same time.

D The ASBO has become a badge of pride – you are not regarded as tough if you don't have one.

E ASBOs have stopped a lot of bad behaviour and made some areas much safer places.

F They can start young people on the road to becoming a criminal. If they break an ASBO, they could go to court and get a criminal record. They might not have done anything really serious.

G The trouble with dispersal of groups is that all young people suffer even when they are not causing trouble.

H I should have the right to meet my friends where I like without the police moving us on.

I The Mosquito drives all young people away when they are not causing any trouble.

J The Mosquito is a good way of moving on large groups of young people who intimidate older people and shoppers without involving the police. It stops trouble happening.

K It is not fair to cause actual pain to our hearing when some adults just want to get us out of the way.

A different approach

Some people believe these measures are the wrong way to control anti-social behaviour. They look for more positive approaches – ways of engaging young people or working out problems with them. The government is looking at early intervention schemes where help is given to a family much earlier on if problems are identified.

DISCUSS

Look at the ideas on the right. Which of them do you think are the most likely to work? Choose your top two and justify your choice. Or come up with some ideas of your own.

- Opening youth clubs
- Access to a sports centre
- Coffee bars or similar places where young people can meet and talk at night
- Encouraging young people to meet older people
- Youth forum where young people can meet councillors, the police or other people in authority to show their side of things
- A skate park
- Youth shelters where young people can meet without being hassled

Read the scenario on the right. Then write speech bubbles to say what you think the following people might say about whether ASBOs and/or dispersal of groups should be used. Improvise a role-play drama and act out a conversation between these people on this issue, and what can be done about it to improve matters.

Scenario

There has been a lot of trouble in the town centre where large noisy groups of young people meet during the day and at night. They are drinking a great deal, fighting and causing damage. Some older people and parents with their children are almost too scared to come into the centre to shop and businesses are complaining.

Older resident who has lived in the town all his life, is fed up with anti-social behaviour and wants it stopped

Young person who meets her friends in groups in town but has never been in any trouble

Parents with young children

Police officer who wants a straightforward way of dealing with the problem but does not want to antagonise young people

Local councillor who wants a solution but wants to satisfy both older and young people

Business person who is concerned about the problems the behaviour is causing for local businesses but wants to help young people stop this behaviour

Developing your arguing skills

If you want to persuade people of your point of view (rather than just shout at them) then you have to develop a convincing argument. You have to 'make a case' for the ideas you are putting forward. Making a case means that you make a number of points that are supported by reasons and, if possible, some evidence. The points should be clearly related to the issue you are discussing and should build on each other.

Activity

1 Look at the arguments below. There are three key points which argue the case that ASBOs are a good way of stopping anti-social behaviour. There are also three supporting paragraphs and evidence.
   a) Identify the three key points.
   b) Match a supporting paragraph to each of the points.
   c) Decide in what order you would put the points (and their paragraphs) to make the case most effectively.
2 Make a case against ASBOs, dispersal orders or Mosquitoes. Alternatively, you could make a case for more positive ways of preventing anti-social behaviour.

A In Nottingham a family moved into Shirley Fenn's street. Two of the boys in the family held all-night parties, left rubbish in neighbours' gardens, damaged property, and threatened and harassed anybody who complained. Two ASBOs were granted. At first the boys treated them as a badge of honour. But when one of the boys continued the same behaviour, he was taken to court and told that he would get a custodial sentence if he carried on. The bad behaviour stopped and life in the street has improved enormously (Home Office website).

B Yobbish behaviour that is threatening or disturbing can occur in any town centre or even your own neighbourhood. ASBOs are a tool that help communities take back their streets. They prevent areas becoming worse and more lawless.

C There are examples where ASBOs have been successful and bring relief to communities.

D They give a young person a chance to think about and change their behaviour before they get into worse trouble with the police, get arrested and end up with a criminal record.

E ASBOs help protect a community from people who try to make the lives of others miserable.

F Another advantage of ASBOs is that they act as a warning to young people.

1.2 Why do young people break the law?

No one of any age is allowed to break the law. But in England, Wales and Northern Ireland the age of criminal responsibility is ten (eight in Scotland). It is thought that children younger than this probably do not understand that what they have done is wrong. If they commit a serious crime, social services will deal with the case. Everyone over the age of ten is held responsible for their crimes and can be arrested, tried and, if found guilty, punished.

A At the end of the day I still think it was me … But little things just push you in one direction or just help you along your way.

B It's all about who you grow up with … If you grew up in a rough area, with all people doing crime, smoking dope and whatever, doing drugs, the kids that grew up in that area, they've got a bigger chance that they'll end up like that as well.

C [I was] slung out of my house at eleven years of age, no mum to love me, no brothers, nothing … It's the love that your family has to give you that can stop [you offending], nothing else. If your mum and dad shows you neglect, I guarantee you you're going into crime.

D On the street you're looking for a hard reputation …

E Kids hang out in groups, some of them are criminals already, and they dare them to do a house robbery or something like that … so they end up going to do it and they get lucky and get away with it … if they think they can earn about £1000 by doing a house or two … not a likely chance of getting caught, so why not?

F Problems at home led me to hang around street corners. I got into drugs, I didn't have any money so I started stealing, then I got on to car theft, things like that.

These quotes are adapted from *Wasted Lives* published by the crime reduction charity Nacro.

Activity

1 Read the quotes on this page. What do they tell you about the reasons why some young people get into trouble?
2 Look at the list of reasons on page 9 that have been suggested as to why young people break the law. Which of them match the quotes on page 8?
3 Working in small groups, decide:
   a) which five you think are the most important reasons that lead young people towards crime
   b) if you would add any others.
4 Create your class's top five reasons. Be prepared to justify the ones your group chose.

Reasons why young people break the law

Not getting on well at school

Feeling unloved or unhappy

No skills

Harsh discipline

Parents split up

Parents unable to control them

Drugs/ alcohol

Influenced by friends

No respect for other people

Come from a poor family

History of crime in the family

Bored

Excluded from school

Trying to impress other young people

Looking for attention

Feeling that they are not respected

DISCUSS

1 Some people have suggested that many young people don't know right from wrong and see nothing wrong with criminal activity, even if it hurts other people. How far do you agree with this?

2 Do you think the age of criminal responsibility should be put higher or lower than ten? Below are some arguments to help you think about this. Justify your opinion.

Age of criminal responsibility in other countries	
Canada	12
France	13
Germany	14
Italy	15
Spain	16

- Children under ten are too young to know what they are doing.
- Children under ten do know right from wrong. They know when they are committing a crime.

- Treating young children who do bad things as people who need help is better for them and for society. I would raise the age to twelve.
- If you let them get away without a proper punishment they will just go on to worse crimes. I'd make the age eight.

9

Gangs have attracted a lot of attention in the newspapers and on television. They seem to lead their members into crime and have been held responsible for violent and anti-social behaviour, particularly involving the use of knives. There has been talk of 'postcode' gangs where young people can get into difficulties if they go into another gang's area. So why are so many people interested in joining gangs?

Read this article, which was written for Headliners by four young people: Jaclyn Adu-Sarkode (12), Nataleigh Taylor (15), Alysha Lonergan (11) and Samsam Farah (15) from west London.

HEADLINERS

S > MAKING NEWS CHANGING LIVES > MAKING NEWS CHANGING LIVES > MAKING NEWS CHANGING LIVES > MAKING NEWS CHA

Gangs: What's the attraction?

Peer pressure and wanting to look 'bad' are two of the reasons, but during our investigation, one thing seemed to stand out. Young people are searching for some kind of family unit.

Chris Saed is a youth worker at Sulgrave Youth Club, a place that gives young people something to do during the weeknights and keeps them from falling into things like gangs:

"I think what gangs offer you in comparison to a family are security and protection. Being in a gang means you always have someone watching your back, and people that feel they don't have that protection and support at home will look elsewhere for it."

Michael is another youth worker:

"There are many reasons why young people get into gangs. The main reason is just to have friends. Peer pressure can lead people into a situation where there is a need to feel like you belong to something. It can seem like a family, not all families are good though, but some are. It depends on what your gang does. You could be in a gang that helps old people across a road. A youth club is a gang but not a negative one."

Once you're in a gang it can be hard to break free. But 22-year-old Kemar did:

"At the time I was a kid, a gang was just being bad, troubling people, not to the full extent of stabbing someone but obviously harming them. Punching or kicking them, belittling them in front of people.

"We didn't have guns or knives. We were actually scared to use knives. It was only a few that used knives to make a big point, and this isn't going back too long ago. But we were scared most of the time. We weren't troublemakers, we were just doing it to fit in.

"I doubt gangs will fade away. People always want to fit in and even if it's in the bad or wrong crowd or the right crowd, people just want to fit in.

"A friend of mine is in prison. He's older than me but he's in a gang and he's still got that gang mentality. I managed to get out but he stayed in, and now he's in prison for stabbing someone and really truly it was over nothing, it was over status. The guy said, 'oh I'm badder than you', so he stabbed him. Now that's it. His life is screwed up. If he comes out he can't get a job, he can't have a proper life.

"If any young person came to me for advice, I'd just tell them don't go into a gang. Seriously, gangs are just not worth it. Because when you reach my age you won't have anything to look back on, or nothing to live off. You won't have education, you won't have a job, you won't have money."

It seems that gangs come in different shapes and forms and not all are bad. Some are there to support and back up kids and teens like families. But choose the gang you pick carefully, because you could be getting into a sticky situation.

Source: www.headliners.org

DISCUSS

1 Do you agree with the opinions in the article about gangs?
2 Why is it difficult in some areas for young people to avoid joining a gang?
3 Are gangs always a bad thing?

Activity

Either

Write your own article in the same style as this one about gangs and why young people join them. This could be relevant to the particular area you live in.

Or

Write a short magazine article setting out the advice you would give young people about gangs and how they can try to ensure they remain safe in an area where there are gangs.

1.4 What happens to young offenders when they are caught?

The UK youth justice system uses three main ideas when dealing with offenders:

1 They should **take responsibility** for what they have done.
2 They should **make amends** to the victims of the crime or to the community.
3 They should be **given help** to get back on the right track and stop offending.

How the youth justice system works for young people aged ten to seventeen

Who decides	What you get
Police The police decide whether to give a reprimand or a final warning. 	**Informal warning** If a young person commits a first, minor offence, they might get an informal warning or 'telling off'. Or a **Reprimand (an official telling-off)** This is given at the police station with an appropriate adult present if the young person admits their guilt. This goes on the young person's criminal record.
Youth Offending Team (YOT) The YOT is made up of members of the police and social services, and education, probation and health agencies in a local area. 	Or a **Final warning** If the offence is more serious, or the young person has been in trouble before, they will be given a final warning. This means they will be referred to a Youth Offending Team. The team decides what action needs to be taken to stop the young person from offending again.
Youth Court This is a special court for young people, heard by magistrates. 	**Youth Court** If the offence is serious, or it is a second or third offence, the person will be charged and sent straight to a Youth Court for trial. The magistrates decide whether the young person is guilty, and if so, what the punishment should be. If the offender is under ten there will be no trial, but the Youth Court will be asked to make a Child Safety Order.

Activity

What do you think should happen to each of the offenders below? Should they:

• get a reprimand
• receive a final warning
• be sent to the Youth Court?

Think about how old each offender is, what they have done and how serious the offence is.

Asif is eleven years old and has been getting into trouble a lot at school. He was seen on camera damaging cars in the school car park. This is not his first case of vandalism. He is well-known on his estate for breaking windows and getting into fights.

Michael is thirteen and has been arrested for stealing from a shop. He has not been in trouble before and his role in this offence was fairly minor – he was the look-out. The other three involved were older boys who persuaded him to go along. He admits his guilt.

Greta is fourteen and has been found in possession of drugs – mostly pills. The police suspect that she has been supplying them to other young people. Greta has been excluded from school for persistent bad behaviour and rudeness to teachers.

Trevor is sixteen and has stolen an elderly woman's handbag in the street, pushing her to the ground. He already has a final warning from the police for theft. His parents are not able to control Trevor and say he has got in with a bad lot of friends. He has not responded to the programme of the Youth Offending Team in connection with his final warning.

Marcie is sixteen and the mother of a small boy aged six months. She was caught shoplifting from a clothes store. It is her first offence. She says she has no money to buy clothes and wanted something for a party. She is worried that the baby will be put into care if she is taken into custody.

Winston is sixteen. He has been arrested for taking a vehicle and driving it away with a group of friends. They had all been drinking heavily. This is his first offence and he says he is sorry.

The Youth Offending Team

If a young person gets a final warning, they are referred to a Youth Offending Team (YOT). Usually one member of the team will take responsibility for the young person, although two or three other members of the team may also be involved. They will draw up a programme for the young person.

The programme will try to change the young person's attitudes and behaviour. It might cover things like:

- reasons why the young person got into trouble
- help for parents to control the young person better
- counselling for the young person
- community activities
- an apology to the victim and repair of any damage
- improving school work and attendance.

The programme is not a punishment. It is meant to stop the young person re-offending.

This is a made-up programme for John Green who has been caught causing criminal damage by spraying graffiti on walls. He has also been in fights in school and his teachers say he can't control himself.

Programme:

- Attend three sessions with a YOT worker, looking at the consequences of his actions.
- Attend group sessions on anger management.
- Assist a local community group that is preparing a mural in a local youth club.

The Youth Offending Team might be made up of:

police officers	a youth worker
social workers	a probation officer
a teacher	a mental health nurse.
a magistrate	

Activity

Work in small groups as if you were a Youth Offending Team. Look at the two cases below and draw up suitable programmes for the two young people to help them stop offending and have more successful lives.

Michael is thirteen and has been arrested for being involved in stealing DVDs from a shop. Three older boys were involved and persuaded him to go along.

He has not been in trouble before. He says he is sorry and promises not to get into trouble again.

Michael's father recently left the family after rows with Michael's mother. Michael hasn't seen his father for a few months. Michael has become friendly with a group of older boys who have left school or dropped out early. All of the older boys have been in trouble with the police. He has been truanting from school and does not go out with his old school friends any more. Michael's teachers say he was doing very well and could get good exam results if he applies himself. He has lost confidence in his ability to succeed at school. His mother says she is finding it difficult to get him to do what she says.

Ling is sixteen. She has been involved in criminal activity, including shoplifting cosmetics and using illegal drugs. She is involved with a gang of girls doing similar things. The gang has also caused quite a lot of damage to the local community, although the police are not sure whether Ling has been involved in this.

Ling appears to be on the fringes of the gang and has shown the desire to stop committing offences. Her parents are horrified that she has got involved in criminal activities, and do not know how to go about changing her behaviour. Ling has dropped out of school and there is little chance of her doing her GCSEs.

If young people commit a serious offence, or if they reoffend after a final warning, the case goes to a Youth Court. The Youth Court is a type of magistrates' court specially designed for young people under the age of eighteen. It is less formal than adult courts; the magistrates are specially trained, and they have a different range of sentences they can pass. The cases are held in private: members of the public are not allowed in. The parents of the young person are generally expected to attend.

Magistrates

Two or three magistrates sit behind a big desk (the bench). They are men and women chosen from the community (not lawyers) who decide whether the young person has committed the offence and how they are going to be dealt with. Most magistrates are not paid. One of the magistrates (usually the one in the middle) is the chairperson and speaks for them all.

Witness

A police officer might give details of the offence, or another person might say what happened. Witnesses only attend if the young person says he or she is not guilty.

Usher

The usher calls in the witnesses and keeps out members of the public, who are not allowed to be present.

Youth Offending Team (see page 14)

Some of the team might attend. They sit at the back of the court.

Young person, parents and solicitor

The young person who is charged with the offence (the defendant) sits in the middle of the court in front of the bench. The parents sit on one side and a solicitor usually sits on the other. The solicitor is a trained lawyer who knows the law and is there to protect the legal rights of the young person.

Justice's clerk
The clerk sits at the side or in front of the magistrates. The clerk is a trained lawyer and advises the magistrates on the law. The clerk is responsible for the day-to-day running of the court. The clerk reads out the charge (the offence the young person is said to have committed) and asks whether he/she pleads guilty or not. The clerk has no say in deciding whether the young person is guilty, and does not decide what should happen to them, although he/she may tell the magistrates what alternatives are open to them.

Prosecutor
The prosecutor is a solicitor whose job is to set out the case against the young person for the police. The prosecutor provides the evidence to show that the person committed the offence.

Victim
Victims may come to court if they wish, and may be involved before the magistrates decide on any sentence.

Activity

Mock youth court
You are going to hold a trial in a youth court. You will need members of the class to play the roles of the three magistrates, the justice's clerk, the prosecutor, a police officer, the defendant, the usher, witnesses, the defendant's parents, members of the YOT.

Follow the Youth Court procedure on page 18 during the trial and use the boxes on page 19 to help you. You will need to improvise and make up elements of the case.

You will need some to time to prepare your ideas. The witnesses and lawyers can use the police statement on page 18 to work out what they are going to say, and make up the rest. Other members of the class could help them, for example two students could help each lawyer.

The case
Three boys are accused of being involved in stealing an MP3 player from another boy. One of the boys is directly accused of taking it and the others of helping him.

Youth Court procedure

1 The clerk reads out the charges and checks that the young person understands what the charges mean.
2 The young person (defendant) pleads 'guilty' or 'not guilty'.
3 If the defendant pleads 'not guilty', the case proceeds.
4 The prosecutor sets out the case against the defendant and calls witnesses for the prosecution, starting with the arresting officer for the police. The defence lawyer cross-examines these witnesses.
5 The defence calls witnesses to support its case, starting with the defendant. The prosecution cross-examines these witnesses.
6 After all the evidence has been heard, the magistrates decide whether the defendant is guilty or not.
7 If the defendant is found guilty, the magistrates pass sentence.
8 The magistrates can ask the Youth Offending Team to prepare a report on the offender if they do not feel they have enough information to pass sentence.

Arresting officer's statement

'I was patrolling the area around Beeston shopping centre in the High Road at 4.15p.m. on 3 May when I was called over by a Mrs Rolph, 47, who said that she had found a young man in a distressed state who had had his MP3 player stolen from him. When I questioned the young man, Josh Greely (14), he said that three youths had threatened him and taken his music player. He gave me a description of the youths. A colleague joined me in searching the surrounding area and we came on the three youths: Kevin Eylett (16), Adrian Studley (16) and Kedi Odrah (15). We searched them and found an MP3 player on Kevin. This matched the one described by Josh Greely. We detained the youths and took them to the police station where they were later charged.'

Josh Greely's statement

'I was just walking on my way home when I was stopped by three boys. I was listening to my MP3 player. One of them (identified as Kevin Eylett) spoke very quietly to me in a threatening manner. He said that he wanted the player and was going to have it. He told me to hand it over or I would get a beating. He flashed something metal that I thought was a knife. There were two boys with him, they looked tough. I was very frightened, so I handed over my player. After this, Mrs Rolph came up to me and called the police.'

On this page are details of the witnesses, the lawyers and some of the other people in the trial. You are given some idea of what they will say, but you have to make up exactly what they do say. You can add information or any other ideas of your own. You can increase the number of witnesses, but no more than four for each side.

Witnesses

Prosecution

1 Josh Greely (see his statement on page 18).
2 Mrs Rolph – says that she saw the three boys around Josh and that they looked suspicious. She says that two of the boys were acting like look-outs. She did not actually see them take the MP3 player, but she saw that Josh was very upset.
3 A friend of Josh, Bill Humble, says that he can identify the MP3 player as belonging to Josh.

Defence

1 Kevin says the MP3 player had been given to him a long time ago, and there are lots like it around. He says that he had spoken to Josh because Josh had been giving him a dirty look, so he decided to have a word with him.
2 The other two defendants, Adrian Studley and Kedi Odrah, support this story. They say they were not really interested in what was going on and had nothing to do with any theft.
3 Jake Morris, known to the defendants, who was passing at the time says that he saw the boys and nothing was going on.

Lawyers

Your job is to try to prove the case for your side. You need to ask questions to challenge what the other side is saying. You will have to listen carefully to the witnesses, because they may say things not mentioned on the left.

Prosecution

You have to prove that the three boys are guilty. Set out the case against them, and use your witnesses to show what happened.

Defence

You have to prove that the boys are innocent. You must challenge the stories of the prosecution witnesses, and make the magistrates believe your side's account.

Justice's clerk and usher

Your roles are set out on pages 16–17. The usher asks the witnesses to swear the oath: 'I do solemnly, sincerely and truly declare and affirm that the evidence I shall give shall be the truth, the whole truth, and nothing but the truth.'

Magistrates

You are in control of the court and will decide if all or some of the defendants are guilty. Remember – the guilt of the person(s) has to be proven beyond reasonable doubt.

1.6 Sentencing

What is the purpose of sentencing?

To help offenders be better citizens and stop offending

To give criminals what they deserve – punishment!

To deter others from offending

What is the purpose of sentencing?

To make victims feel they have received justice

To make the community a safer place

Activity

How good do you think you would be at deciding what sentence an offender should receive? Work in groups of four: three will be the magistrates, one an observer. Draw your own sentencing and observation sheets like those on page 22. The magistrates should discuss each case, decide what they are trying to achieve (look at the purposes of sentencing above), then decide on the sentence and give their reasons for it. You will then write down what your sentence is on the sheet and your reasons for giving it.

The observer will make notes on the observation sheet. There are four cases, so each person gets a turn at being the observer. At the end, you will feed back your thoughts to each other on how well you've done.

The cases

A Sarah, fifteen years old, has been found guilty of stealing £40 from an old lady who lives on her estate. She has helped the old lady at times, doing small jobs for her, but this time she took the money from her purse.

B Jasmina, seventeen, has been convicted for selling drugs, mainly cannabis and ecstasy. She deals to feed her own drug habit. She has also been arrested before for petty theft. She is living in a flat with friends. She has no parents, and was brought up in a children's home.

C Billy has been found guilty of robbery with assault. He stole goods and money from a small store. With two accomplices, he also beat and kicked the storekeeper who tried to stop him. Billy has a violent history of being involved in fights in the local area. His father was violent to him when he was a child.

D Kenneth has been part of a gang stopping school students on the way home from school and taking their money and mobile phones. They never hurt anybody because the victims were too frightened to do anything.

Sentences

You can give a combination of orders. This means you might award a compensation order, a reparation order and a supervision order for a particular offender.

- **A fine**

- **Compensation order**
  Money paid to victim, usually up to £1000.

- **Reparation order**
  This means putting things right. It could involve repairing damage, writing an apology, or meeting the victim face to face to talk about the crime.

- **Action plan order**
  Can require offenders to:
  – join anger management classes or drug/alcohol misuse programmes
  – present themselves at particular times at specified places
  – go to an attendance centre for a certain number of hours
  – stay away from specified places, for example shopping centres
  – carry out work of benefit to the community, for example clean a local canal.

- **Custodial order**
  Offenders over fifteen can be sent to a young offenders' institution for a period of time. Alternatively (especially for younger offenders), half the sentence is spent in a local authority secure unit or training centre and half under supervision in the community.

- **Attendance order**
  Report to a centre, usually run by police, for two hours twice a month for between 12 and 36 hours.

- **Supervision order**
  The offender is supervised by a social worker, probation officer or another member of a YOT for between three months and three years.

- **Parenting order**
  Parents are told by the court to have greater control over their child. The parents may have to attend parenting classes to learn how to do this. A fine of £1000 is made if the parents do not agree to do this.

DISCUSS

1 Take each case in turn on page 20 and discuss the sentences given by different groups. Use these questions to help you:

- What sentence was given?
- Did the magistrate give good reasons for their sentence?
- What did the sentence seek to achieve for the offender?
- Did the sentence consider the victims?
- How difficult was it to reach a sentence that was fair?

At the end of each case, agree in the class what the fairest sentence is.

2 Why do you think sentences should be given?

3 Do you want to punish criminals hard and make the victims feel better, or do you think the sentence should in some way help the criminal back into society?

4 In what order of importance would you put the purposes of sentencing in the diagram on page 20?

Sentencing sheet

What sentence are you giving?
(Remember, you can give a combination of orders.)

What are your reasons for giving this sentence?

Observation sheet

Case	Names of magistrates
Are they listening to each other?	
Is everybody contributing to the discussion?	
Are they co-operating in coming to a decision?	
Are they prepared to negotiate and compromise?	
Can they justify the sentence they are giving?	

1.7 The consequences of crime

Every crime, however small, has consequences. Most crimes have victims who suffer loss or injury, sometimes affecting them for the rest of their lives. There may be serious consequences for the offender, whose life may be changed by being caught. But there also consequences for all of us in different ways:

- fear of crime, which can deeply affect some people's lives
- the cost in money and time, in health costs if a person is hurt or injured
- insurance costs for theft and damage
- the costs of the emergency services – police, fire and ambulance.

DISCUSS

What are the consequences for the people involved in the crime shown below? How do you think they will be affected in the future?

John and Millicent Martin have been burgled. Their life savings, around £5000, have been taken. The burglars caused a lot of damage. The two boys who carried out the burglary have been caught. However, they have spent the money, mainly on drugs, clothes and gadgets.

The victims

" I don't understand why they did this to us. We haven't got much. That £5000 had to last us for the rest of our lives. We can get by on our pension, but that money was for little extras, and to pay for major things like a new washing machine. They've taken our memories — things we can never get back — like Uncle Albert's clock, our daughter's wedding photo in a silver frame, and John's medals. He nearly died for those, fighting for this country — they meant so much to him. I don't think we'll ever feel safe in this house again. "

Insurance costs

John and Millicent had some insurance, which will pay for the damage and a little towards the things they've lost, but these were not particularly valuable. It will only cover money stolen from the house up to £500. All in all the company will pay out £2500.

The burglars

Graham Watson and Asif Ahmed, both seventeen years old, were each sentenced to eighteen months at a young offenders' institution, since they had been involved in other offences for which they received non-custodial sentences. Graham will not be able to continue his course at college and Asif has lost his job in a photographer's shop.

Justice costs

- Cost of Youth Court time including work of legal officers (difficult to estimate but several thousand pounds)
- Cost of custodial sentence – over £30,000 each.

Activity

Read about the crime opposite, and on a blank sheet of paper complete the consequences boxes. Use the questions as a guide.

Insurance costs

These have been done for you. Both cars were a write-off:

- Family car – £8000
- Stolen car – £4500
- Clearing up accident and taking away cars – £1200
- Council repairs to road and kerb damage – £600

Other members of their family

How might they be affected?

John and Chelsea

What might happen to John and Chelsea in the youth court, and how might this affect their future?

John, aged sixteen and Chelsea, aged fifteen, took a car for a joy ride. They were spotted by the police and there was a chase. Coming round a bend, John lost control and hit a car that was carrying a family and their young child. The father was badly injured with broken bones and internal injuries, but the wife got away with a broken arm, and the baby had bruises and a cracked rib. John and Chelsea were shocked but not hurt.

Emergency services' costs and time

What sorts of things would the ambulance, fire and police be involved in as a result of the crash?

(You will not be able to give costs.)

The victims

How might the crash affect the family's:

- health

- mental state

- income

- father's job

- mother's job?

Medical costs

What would the National Health Service have to pay for as a result of the accident?

Activity

Working in pairs or threes, choose two of the crimes below and draw up lists of consequences, like the ones on these pages.

- Hurting someone badly in a fight.
- Taking drugs.
- Vandalism on a railway line or motorway.
- Mugging people in the street.

If a young offender is over the age of fifteen, he or she can be sentenced to custody in a young offenders' institution (YOI). What is it like inside? What experiences do the young people have? Does it help them, or does it turn them into hardened criminals?

The views below are compiled from interviews with several young people who have spent quite a lot of time in YOIs. Most of them have long records of offending, stretching back to the ages of twelve and thirteen. What they have in common now is the desire not to spend any more time in prison.

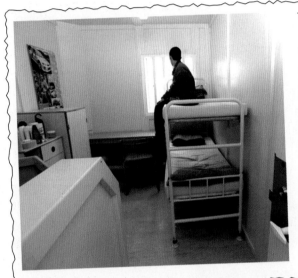

What are YOIs like inside?

'The YOIs in old prisons can be dirty, paint peeling off walls and the like. Others are modern or have been done up and are all right. The cells are small and usually you share. Apart from a double bunk bed you have a table, a washbasin and metal chairs fixed to the wall – not much else. You can have a radio and a CD player. But whatever the cells are like it does your head in to be stuck in them for so long each day. The boredom is a real killer.'

What's the daily routine like?

'It varies with the institution. In some of them you're banged up in your cell for over eighteen hours a day and you get very little exercise and not much association time – that's mixing with other inmates. In other places you're banged up for less time, fifteen to sixteen hours. You get more leisure time, say two hours' association time every evening, one hour's exercise, two hours' education, and so on. But you often spend a lot of time in your cell. In some places you can get jobs and earn some money (not much) gardening, in the kitchens, or as a landing cleaner. You can spend that on your canteen. Once a week you are given your money, about £2.50, and you can spend it on tobacco, sweets, that kind of thing.'

What are the worst things about being inside?

'You don't know what's going on outside. Say you've got trouble with your family. It only takes one person to say something and, together with everything else that's in your head, it makes you feel bad and frustrated because you can't do anything. Also with girlfriends there's so much stress; you think she's out clubbing; she's seeing someone; you feel paranoid because you don't know what's going on – it drives you mad … And there's never enough food! You're always hungry … And the boredom!

There's a lot of violence and bullying. In prison you've got nothing, so things mean something. I've seen a fight over a packet of biscuits. Whenever somebody has something, others think they should have a share. And there'll always be someone who takes it all to show how hard they are. If you go round the cells in a prison, there will always be people who can't fight to save their lives. But they can survive in jail by bartering: swap something; sell something; do things for people. You can feel very threatened. Once I never came out of my cell much for two weeks because five lads were waiting to get me. I sat in my cell with a chair leg ready to have a go. Eventually, I got myself put into solitary and then got shipped out to another YOI.'

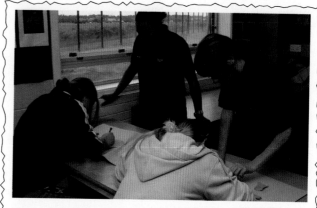

Do YOIs help you to change?

'In some ways they make things worse because you build up a network of new contacts with criminals, people who say "See me when you get out," and they introduce you to their friends and get you drugs, etc. Also you feel so angry and frustrated that when you do get out you're likely to go and get yourself into trouble.

The education – basic maths and English, cooking, computers – is quite useful. But the officers, apart from a few, aren't interested much. You can't blame them, they're just doing a job, and most of the inmates don't want help, they just want to do their time and get out and go back to their old life. In three and a half years only one officer, a female officer, has been really helpful and tried to encourage me to change when I leave prison. You need much more advice about how to get jobs, and more help to find places to live and start again in a new place. Because if you go back to where you were you just slip into your old ways.'

Activity

All YOIs are inspected regularly. Some of the things inspectors look at are:

- prisoners' everyday lives (for example, accommodation, visits, education)
- custody and control (for example, bullying, security, use of restraint)
- care and resettlement (for example, community activities, release)
- the building and facilities.

What recommendations would you make to improve young offenders' institutions, from the information that you have read on these two pages?

Reflection

How well do you think you're doing?
  Think back over the work you have done in Section 1.

Skills

- Draw a chart like the one below, and give yourself a grade from 1 to 5, where 1 is the lowest and 5 is the highest.
- Give evidence for your score and say how you could improve your skills.

Assessing your progress
In this section you will be assessing how well you can:

- give your opinion and explain it to others
- listen to and take other people's opinions into account
- make a case for a point of view
- make decisions
- decide what you think is fair
- understand issues to do with youth crime and justice.

How well can you ... ?	1	2	3	4	5	Evidence for your score?	How can you improve?
give your opinions							
explain your opinions							
listen to and take other people's opinions into account							
make a case for a point of view							
make decisions							

Understanding

- Complete the following sentences:
  'The main ideas behind the UK youth justice system are …'
  'The main purposes of sentencing are …'
- How fair is the law to young people?
- What do you understand by the following?
  reprimand   *Youth Offending Team*   *ASBOs*
          Final Warning   *Youth Court*
- Talk to another pupil and discuss what you think was the most important thing you learned in this section.

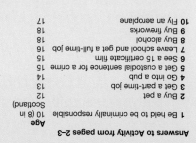

Answers to Activity from pages 2–3

Age

1 Be held to be criminally responsible — 10 (8 in Scotland)
2 Buy a pet — 12
3 Get a part-time job — 13
4 Go into a pub — 14
5 Get a custodial sentence for a crime — 15
6 See a 15 certificate film — 15
7 Leave school and get a full-time job — 16
8 Buy alcohol — 18
9 Buy fireworks — 18
10 Fly an aeroplane — 17

11 Give consent to heterosexual and homosexual activity — 16
12 Marry with parent's consent — 16 (without consent 18 in Scotland)
13 Buy cigarettes and tobacco — 18
14 Join the armed forces — 16 (with parent's consent)
15 Play the National Lottery — 16
16 Drive a car — 17
17 Have a tattoo — 18
18 Buy an air rifle — 17

19 Vote — 18
20 Sign a tenancy agreement — 18 (16 in Scotland)
21 Buy a house — 18
22 Leave home without your parents' consent — 18
23 Be entitled to National Minimum Wage (young person's rate) — 18
24 Stand for Parliament — 21
25 Adopt a child — 21
26 Be entitled to the National Minimum Wage (full adult rate) — 22
27 Gamble — 18

Section 2
Local communities and local government

We all live in a local community, or neighbourhood, which might be part of a village, a town, a city, or a borough. Each area has its own local government – the council – which is elected by the people living in that area. The council makes decisions about everyday things and provides services like rubbish collection, libraries, nurseries, council housing, homes for the elderly, schools. Everyone needs to know how the council works, to make sure that they can influence its decisions, and to help make their community a better place to live. Communities are happier, safer places when people get on well together and believe that they are treated fairly.

KEY WORDS

councillor

election

services

community

stereotype

discrimination

Who makes decisions about local matters?

What things help people to get on well with each other?

How can people influence these decisions?

How do people get on in our area?

Assessing your progress
In this section you will be assessing how well you can:

- discuss different ideas, opinions and beliefs
- take account of other people's views
- explain your own opinion and give reasons for it
- plan some action with other people
- understand the issues to do with living in communities, including differences between groups of people.

What do you do if nobody is emptying your dustbins?

What do you do if your neighbours are really noisy and keep you awake?

How can you make the streets look better in the area around your home and where you go to school?

Activity

Work in pairs or threes. The people in the cases opposite have all come to the council for advice and help. But they don't know where to go. Can you help them?

For each of the six cases shown opposite:

a) decide which department the people could go to for help
b) suggest what you think this council department can do, if anything, to help
c) decide what you think would be the best solution to the situation. (This may be not only what the council can do but also what other people can do.)

Use the illustrations of the council on pages 32–33 to find your answers.

The answer to all these questions is – contact your local council! Councils are responsible for many of the services in your local area. Most people want to live in clean, quiet streets where people get on with each other, to have their rubbish collected regularly, and to walk and play in well-kept parks. These services make a big difference to the quality of people's everyday lives. Not all councils provide the same services, but they usually cover the areas shown in the illustrations on pages 32–33.

A **Zoe Bakewell** and her family have had just about enough of their next-door neighbours, the Wilkinsons. During the daytime and into the evening, the Wilkinson children play their music so loud that the Bakewells can hardly hear the television. They come in late at night, sometimes at 2 or 3a.m., and always wake up the Bakewells with their laughter, shouting and swearing.

C **John Costa's** house has been repossessed because he was made redundant, his mortgage has gone up and he could not afford the payments. He has a wife, an aunt and three children living with him. They desperately need accommodation.

B **Ellen Ross** is 85 years old and lives on her pension. She has no other money. She lives on her own in a block of flats. But her neighbours never go to see her to find out if she is all right. She cannot walk very far. She cannot do her shopping and needs someone to help her clean her flat.

E **Shirina and Winston Smith** and several other residents are very concerned about a new office block, which is being built behind their house. They were consulted about the original plans, but the block seems to be much higher than the plans showed. They are sure it is going to make their houses dark and stop them getting sunlight in their gardens. They are also concerned about the noise, dust and dirt coming off the site on to their houses.

D **Jose and Martha Jenkins** cannot pay their council tax bills. They are both over 50 years old and are unable to get work. They get unemployment benefit, but they cannot save enough money to pay the huge council tax bill in one go. If they do not pay their bill, they can be taken to court.

F **Margita Donaghue** has just arrived in the area with her two children. She wants to find out about the local schools her children can go to, and what she has to do to get them in. In their previous school, the children were identified as 'gifted children' with special abilities in maths and sciences. Margita wants them to get the right schooling to help them develop their talents.

DISCUSS

1 When you have worked through all the cases, present your answers to the rest of the class.
2 What do each of these situations tell you about:
   a) the work of the council
   b) why the local council is important to the community
   c) how council decisions can affect people's lives?

Example (for situation E): The council controls planning and new building developments. New buildings can be positive, improving run-down areas, creating jobs or new homes. But this can be negative if people lose old homes, businesses create more traffic, and so on.

You have probably heard about **councillors**. These are people who are elected to make the policy decisions for the council. But there are also **council officers**. They do the day-to-day business of running the council. They organise and run the services that the council provides.

Environmental services

This department is responsible for:
- street cleaning, collection of rubbish and items for recycling
- environmental health, including food safety in restaurants and shops, and pest control
- air quality, noise pollution (for example, noisy neighbours) and noise patrol
- giving licences to pubs, clubs and events
- trading standards – making sure shops are selling safe products and not cheating people
- improving the area – making changes to streets and buildings.

Council chamber

This is where debates are held, votes taken and decisions made.

Leisure and amenities

This department looks after:
- parks and open spaces
- recycling centres
- recreation and sports centres
- libraries
- cemeteries
- youth clubs and schemes for young people.

Planning and technical services

This department is responsible for:
- giving permission for new buildings – houses, flats, offices and other business premises
- housing improvement – when people want to extend or change their houses
- highways, pavements and engineering works – digging up roads for pipes, putting in road humps, etc.
- crime prevention, including closed-circuit television (CCTV) cameras.

Housing

This department is responsible for:
• finding homes or accommodation for people who are homeless
• maintaining houses owned by the council
• providing services on council housing estates.

Finance

This department deals with:
• council tax bills and enquiries
• housing benefits
• council rents.

Education

This department now comes under Children, Schools and Families, but it still usually has a separate heading of Education on council websites. Its job is to:
• help to run schools under the council's control
• give out money to schools in the borough (some of it from central government)
• help to sort out arrangements for children to get places in schools
• give parents advice about schools
• have an education welfare section that handles truancy and arrangements for pupils with special educational needs.

Social care and health

This department is responsible for:
• services for families and children
• adoption and fostering
• care of elderly people
• young people who break the law
• mental health care in the community.

The important decisions about what a council should do in an area are made by elected councillors. You are going to hold an election for a councillor and, as a class, you are going to take on the roles of the people who want to be elected to the council. But first you need to know some more about councils.

How councils are elected

Each council area is divided into wards. The people who live in the wards elect the councillors. In country areas there is usually one councillor for each ward but in cities and towns there are often two or three councillors for each ward. Local elections are held every four years on the first Thursday in May. The party with the most elected councillors is in charge of running the council. Sometimes the party with the most councillors does not have an overall majority, so it has to work with other parties.

Councillors

You must be at least 21 years old and you must live in the area to stand for election as a councillor. Many councillors belong to a political party, for example, Labour, Conservative or Liberal Democrat, but not all councillors belong to the big political parties. Some belong to smaller parties like the Greens and some are independent, which means they don't belong to a party at all. Councillors are not paid, but they receive expenses for attending meetings.

Council officers

Working for the councillors are council officers in the departments that you have read about on pages 32–33. They are full-time paid council officials. Their job is to do the day-to-day work, making sure that the council runs smoothly, according to the policy decisions made by the councillors at their council meetings.

What work does a councillor do?

Full council meetings take place about once a month. Senior council officers attend and the meetings are open to the public.

Councillors hold regular surgeries and meet local people to discuss their problems. These might be problems on an estate, dirty streets or a lack of nurseries.

Most council work is done in committees. A small number of councillors, advised by council officers, meet to discuss the work of particular departments, and make decisions, for example, about planning applications.

Activity

Invite a local councillor to come into school to be interviewed for your school magazine or intranet*. Before he or she comes, you will need to find out more about your local council and councillors.

1 Work in small groups to carry out research. You may need to use the local library or visit the council website. Each group can find out different information from the following list:

  a) What sort of council area do you live in (a borough council, a district council, a unitary council)? What decisions can it make?

  b) Obtain a map of the council wards and find out which ward the school is in and which wards you all live in.

  c) Find out how many councillors there are and when the councillors hold their surgeries (when they meet local people).

2 In small groups, discuss your area and decide which issues concern people most. Which of these would you like to ask your councillor about?

3 As a whole class, decide on a list of questions you would like to ask the councillor. Include questions on the following topics:

- why he/she wants to be a councillor
- what jobs he/she holds in the council
- what sorts of problems he/she deals with on behalf of the ward
- what he/she thinks about the issues you have selected.

(*If you cannot arrange for a councillor to visit, you could email your questions. All councillors have an email address, available on the local council website.)

Who will you vote for?

It is time once again for the local council of Trengarth to be elected (local elections take place on the first Thursday in May, every four years). From the picture below, what problems can you see in Trengarth town centre that a councillor might want to do something about?

Now that you've looked at Trengarth's problems, it's time for the election campaign.

1 Campaign

Work in six groups of four or five people. Each group will be allocated one of the candidates on pages 38–9.

a) Decide who in the group will be the candidate. The other members of the group have to help the candidate prepare for the election.

b) What policies (plans) and arguments to support the candidate are you going to put forward?

c) Design and make a leaflet setting out why your candidate should be elected. Use a computer if possible.

2 Election meeting

The candidate from each group stands in the election. The rest of you are the voters.

Each candidate should hand out their leaflet and make a five-minute presentation to say why they should be elected.

3 The vote

a) Ask your teacher for some copies of this ballot paper. Each voter will need one paper.

b) The voters should indicate their first and second choices by marking crosses in the appropriate boxes on the ballot paper.

c) Count up the crosses at the end. The overall winner is the candidate who got the most '1' votes. The candidate who came second is the one who got the most '1' and '2' votes added together.

Councillors for Riverside Ward	[X] VOTE ONCE IN EACH COLUMN	1st Choice ↓	2nd Choice ↓
1	HARDCASTLE, M.		
2	BONDEL, G.		
3	JACKSON, P.		
4	LEONARD, J.		
5	MALIK, S.		
6	PATEL, N.		

4 After the vote

Discuss these questions:

a) Did you give your vote to the candidate who had the best policies and put their case best?

b) Did you vote for the person you liked best because of their personality?

c) Did you vote for the candidate who came from your group?

d) Which candidate do you think had the best policies?

THE CANDIDATES

You are **N. Patel**. You have lived in the local community all your life, and are well known and respected. There are three issues that are close to your heart and that you want to base the campaign on:

- improving existing housing estates
- cleaning up the town centre
- bringing more jobs into the area for young people.

Add any other local issues you wish to campaign on.

You are **J. Leonard**. You have lived in the area for over ten years. You are a committed environmentalist. You are taking part in the election because of concern about one issue — the building of a road. This will mean:

- the demolition of two streets of houses
- an increase in the amount of traffic
- increased pollution
- the loss of some attractive common land with woods.

You want to stop the road being built. You are also concerned about other environmental issues, such as air and noise pollution, recycling and parkland.

You are **M. Hardcastle**. You moved into the area about three years ago and are an enterprising businessperson. You are very keen on developing the town centre to make it attractive for businesses. You want to:

- see the new road scheme go ahead because it will ease the pressure on the town centre, clear away some unattractive housing and reduce pollution in the centre
- pedestrianise part of the town centre
- persuade shopkeepers to invest in repainting and livening up the outside of their shops
- create jobs in the town.

Add any other local issues you wish to campaign on.

You are **S. Malik** and have lived in the area for over fifteen years. You want to see the area develop its sense of community. The areas you are interested in are:

- community centres for old people who are often on their own
- crêches and playgroups for babies and young children
- reducing crime
- improving local parks.

Add any other local issues you wish to campaign on.

You are P. Jackson, a new arrival in the area — a young enterprising person. You want to see the area livened up, particularly its entertainment facilities. You are interested in:

- licences for clubs
- a new cinema complex with six screens
- new shops in the high street
- cleaning up the streets in the town centre and introducing closed-circuit television cameras to reduce crime.

Add any other local issues you wish to campaign on.

You are **G. Bondel**, an older resident who has always lived in the area. You have served on the council before. You are anxious to see the area improve generally. Your main interests are:

- cutting down traffic and reducing noise and fumes
- getting rid of graffiti and litter in the streets
- improving local libraries and parks
- measures to reduce crime.

Add any other local issues you wish to campaign on.

2.3 Supermarket swoop!
A decision-making role play

Grantborough is a district in a small town. It has almost been swallowed up by the growing city of Lencaster nearby. It has a high street containing a newsagent and sweet shop, a small supermarket, a hardware store, a greengrocer, a hairdresser and a few other shops. The newsagent is also a sub post office. You can see what Grantborough looks like on the map.

There are not many jobs in the area, especially for young people and people who want part-time jobs. People have to travel into the city for work, or go further afield. The area is badly served by public transport, so the main way for people to get to work is by car. The roads are narrow and winding, and there is already traffic congestion in the mornings and evenings because commuters travel through Grantborough to reach the city. However, the area is attractive. There is a large park and the houses are low-rise and pleasant.

Now a huge supermarket chain, Fairdeal, wants to build a large supermarket on a site not far from the high street. The site used to contain a shoe factory, but this has closed down. This is going to have a big effect on life in Grantborough, and a number of people are worried about it. You can see the location of the proposed supermarket on the map.

To City of Lencaster

Dual carriageway

New housing estate

St John's church

Parkland

GRANTBOROUGH

Housing

Housing

Shops

Shops

Housing

Proposed supermarket site

Disused railway line siding

You are going to hold a public meeting about the new development.

1 Roles

a) Different groups in the local community have a variety of views on whether it is a good idea or not. Your class is going to divide into groups to play the roles of the people below:

- supermarket developers, designers and public relations officers (this group should have at least five class members in it)
- shopkeepers
- parents with young children
- residents' association
- elderly people
- environmentalists and conservationists
- councillors.

b) On pages 42–3 you will find a brief for your group. Use the brief to work out your position on the new development. Do you welcome it or not? Or would you welcome it if the developers agreed to certain conditions about how the supermarket should be built?

2 The meeting

a) When you have thought about your position, hold a meeting to discuss the proposal. Your teacher, as the chairperson of a local residents' group, will be in charge of the meeting and ask people to speak in turn.

b) The meeting will start with the developers explaining how they intend to develop the supermarket. You will get the chance to ask the developers questions and to put your point of view. You might be able to persuade them to change the way they are going to develop the supermarket.

c) At the end of the meeting, take a vote to see if you want the supermarket or not.

3 The discussion

Discuss the following issues as a class, if possible with an official from the planning office of your local council:

a) What effects do big developments like supermarkets have on communities? Think about the benefits as well as the disadvantages.

b) In what ways can local people make their voices heard when big developments take place in their area?

Group briefs

Supermarket developers, designers and public relations officers

You are anxious to develop a supermarket on this site. There is no space left in the city and people are increasingly shopping by car on the outskirts of cities. So, your task here is to sell the idea of the supermarket to the local people. You are able to make some changes according to what local people would like to see, but you know that some groups will still be against it. You just have to try and persuade them that it will bring them benefits.

Here are some of the ways in which you could appeal to them:

- jobs – especially part-time ones that might particularly suit women with children, but there will also be full-time jobs in the warehouse and in management
- prices of goods
- access roads
- design of the supermarket to make it fit in with local environment, landscaping, measures to cut down noise
- extra facilities – crèche, restaurant, free or cheap buses, etc.

Work out how you can use these factors. You might even draw a new design for the supermarket.

Shopkeepers

You are very worried about the effects that the supermarket might have on your businesses. You need to:

- think about how it might affect the prices of your goods and the number of your customers
- find out what the supermarket owners are going to put in their new store – are they going to have a full range of goods including, for example, clothes and newspapers?

Prepare a list of questions you want to put to the developers.

Councillors

You think that the supermarket will improve the amenities and services in Grantborough and bring money and jobs into the area. You think it is a good solution for the derelict factory site. But you are elected by the local people and don't want to upset them. You won't vote for the supermarket unless the developers give certain guarantees. Work out what you can ask them to do to improve the area and help the local people concerning:

- a new access road to the supermarket – you want to solve the traffic problems caused by people driving into the city through Grantborough every day
- jobs
- car parking facilities and toilets
- environmental issues
- local businesses.

Prepare questions that you want to ask the developers, particularly about the road.

Residents' association

Your group represents the residents – the people who live in Grantborough. You can see that the supermarket has advantages and disadvantages. The things that might worry you are:

- traffic
- what happens to local shops
- design of the supermarket – what it looks like and how it will fit in with other buildings
- access roads and car parking.

Work out your position. Prepare a list of questions you want to ask the developers and a list of things you would like to see them do to make the supermarket more acceptable to residents.

Elderly people

You represent elderly people who meet regularly at the local pensioners' club. You are very concerned about such a big change to the town. Work out:

- what your main worries and concerns are
- what the benefits of a supermarket would be to your age group
- what you would like to see the supermarket include to make it attractive to you.

Prepare a list of questions you want to ask the developers and a list of things you would like to see them do before you will support the proposal.

Environmentalists and conservationists

You are completely opposed to the supermarket development. There is nothing the developers can say to persuade you to change your mind. So you want to devise some difficult questions for them to answer and make some strong points against the development. Work out what you are going to say about:

- traffic – cars and delivery
- air and noise pollution
- the impact that the supermarket buildings will have on the look of Grantborough
- other damage to the environment (litter, trolleys)
- loss of local shops and damage to the community.

Parents with young children

You have to work out whether this is going to be good for you or not. Some of the things you could discuss are:

- shopping – for example, easier or harder, range of goods available, prices
- jobs
- getting to and from the supermarket
- problems of children on roads.

Prepare a list of questions you want to ask the developers and a list of things you would like to see them do before you will support the proposal.

Who pays for the services?

Who pays for the upkeep of your park?

Who pays the people to collect your rubbish?

Who pays for your library?

The simple answer is – you do! Or rather your parents and guardians do. Every household (with a few exceptions) has to pay Council Tax. The tax is paid to the local council, which provides the services in the area.

How much tax is paid depends on the value of the house or flat that you live in. Each property is put into one of the property bands, which go from A to H. Band A is for smaller properties, and Band H is for very large ones. People who live in council houses and flats pay a proportion of their rent as Council Tax. People who live in rented houses and flats have to pay the Council Tax on the property as if they owned it. If you are the only person living in your property you get a 25 per cent discount off your Council Tax.

Councils also get some money straight from the government.

So how do councils spend their money? The pie chart on the right shows how one council breaks down its spending.

Key
- Education
- Housing
- Social Services
- Highways
- Environment
- Planning & Economic Development
- Culture
- Other Services

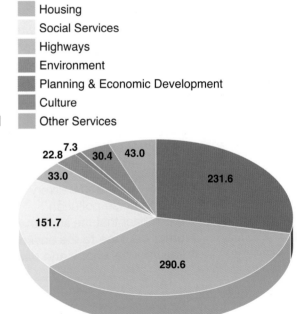

Gross Expenditure £m

Activity

Using the pie chart:

1 What is the biggest proportion of money spent on?

2 What is the second largest amount spent on?

3 Why do you think these categories are so large?

4 What do all the categories tell you about why the council is important to people's lives?

5 Choose one category that you would spend a lot more money on. Explain how you would spend the extra money, and why.

Developing your survey skills

What do you know about the services in your local area?

Work in small groups and think about the services in the area where you live. Divide these up between you, and ask your relatives and neighbours what they think of each of the services you are researching.

How good do they think these services are? Ask your respondents to rate them using the following scale:

1 = terrible 2 = poor 3 = good 4 = very good 5 = excellent

Ask them for their views on how good the services are and put notes on what they say in the third column or on a separate piece of paper.

If you want to add some other services, write them at the bottom of the chart.

(The illustrations of council services at the beginning of this section, on pages 32–3, will help you.)

> The swimming pool could be open earlier at the weekend.

> Our rubbish doesn't get collected on the right day.

> The nurseries are caring and not too expensive.

Services	Do you or your family/neighbours use this service?	How would you rate it on a scale of 1–5?	What have people said about this service?
Rubbish collection			
Schools			
Looking after elderly people • meals • care			
Leisure centres			
Parks			
Childcare/nurseries			
Library			
Noise control			
Recycling centres			
Special events such as firework displays or local fairs			
Car parks			

Activity

When you have done your survey, get together in groups and write up a report on what you've found. Highlight any areas where the service is very poor. Send your report to your local councillor.

How would you spend the money?

You have looked at how you would like to see council money spent. But it is not always as straightforward as it seems.

Activity

1 Work in groups of five or six. You are a council committee that has been given the task of dividing up £200,000 between six competing demands. How are you going to spend the money? Will you allocate most of it to one cause, or are you going to divide it up between several? Which ones are going to lose out?

2 When each group has decided how it is going to divide up the money, get the whole class together and see if you agree. Argue in favour of your group's decisions. This means you have to justify them.

3 What do you think this exercise tells you about the problems councils face having to decide how the money they have collected should be spent?

A Speed bumps

Two streets are regularly being used as 'rat runs' by motorists trying to avoid traffic jams. They are speeding down the streets, ignoring whatever signs you have put up. Two children have been killed in the past two years and several people injured. You could install speed bumps and chicanes to slow the cars down. This will cost £100,000.

B Playground

The local park is in a poor state. There are now many parents with young children in the area. They could really do with some new playground equipment: a slide, swings and a sandpit. This will cost £80,000.

C Library

The library needs some new children's books, some CDs and DVDs. They estimate that the cost will be £20,000.

D School roof

The roof on a local primary school is causing a great deal of concern. For some time it has been letting in rain. The council building unit has had a look at it and says there is a danger it will collapse. Repairs to make it safe and last for about five years would cost £40,000. Or it could be replaced for £90,000 and last for the next 40–50 years.

E CCTV cameras

There have been a lot of robberies in the high street quite near to the town hall. These include attacks on several old people after they had collected their pensions. The police say that CCTV cameras would dramatically reduce this problem. To install these cameras and link them to screens in the police station will cost £60,000.

F Plastic recycling

Too much rubbish is being put into landfill. This is bad for the environment and also very expensive for the council. There is a landfill tax that they have to pay on every tonne of rubbish. At a cost of £40,000, the council could introduce collection and recycling of all waste plastic.

Local councils don't just provide services. They also try to make sure their area is safe and harmonious – a place where people meet up, share common interests, get to know each other and get on together, despite their differences.

In some areas of the country, there is a mixture of people from many different parts of the world. Some of these people were born in Britain and are British, and it is their parents or grandparents who came here years ago.

When people with different customs, languages and traditions live in the same area, they often do not meet each other. They tend to mix only with people like themselves. This can lead to misunderstandings and possible conflict, as in the examples on the next page.

Activity

Look at the three communities on the page opposite where people seem not to get on very well.

Work in pairs.

Read the descriptions of the three communities and look carefully at the illustrations that go with them. Then look at the list below and
a) decide which of these issues apply to the different communities (some apply to more than one)
b) explain their impact on each community.

Lack of facilities for young people

Newcomers

People not mixing

Not enough work in area

Cost of housing

Different religions and customs

Type of housing

Violence and fear of crime and violence

Inequalities of wealth (rich and poor)

DISCUSS

1 Are there similar problems in your community, where different groups do not mix or are uneasy together?
2 Pool your ideas in class discussion about the sorts of problems and issues that arise in mixed areas.

Little Chifford is a village in a beautiful part of the countryside, near the sea. Rich people from other parts of the country have bought cottages here as second homes. They come at weekends and in the summer. They don't really mix with the locals. Local people can't afford to buy houses in the village, and they blame the second-home owners for pushing up prices. Most young people leave to work in nearby towns. Farmers in the area can't get anyone to do work in their fields, and so they employ seasonal foreign workers, who often live in caravans. They don't mix with the locals either, and the local people are not friendly. There have been some fights between the foreign workers and the local youth.

Brantborough is a borough in a large city. There are several large housing estates where many of the poorest families live. There is very little for young people who live on the estates to do, so they often meet each other outside and hang about talking, smoking and drinking. Older people on the estate are frightened of these big groups of young people. They don't go out at night, and they put bars on their doors to protect themselves. The young people get involved in vandalism and fights. Parents are worried that their children will be injured or killed. Everyone seems to be frightened – the old, the young and the parents.

Swatton is an old industrial town that used to produce cloth in large mills. At its busiest, many workers were needed, and people came from abroad to work in the mills. Cheap cloth can now be imported and the industry has died. The mills have been done up and are apartment blocks or business premises. The immigrant workers have settled, found other work and had children and grandchildren. The groups don't mix much and the town now has two different groups who live in different parts of the town, have different religions, follow different customs, eat different foods, etc. There are sometimes disagreements between the groups, often because one group thinks that the others are getting better treatment from the council.

What can be done to help communities get along better?

Activity

Look at this imaginary community. It has plenty of housing but no facilities. Imagine that a mixture of people are going to move in – old people, young families, single people, all of different ethnic backgrounds and with different traditions and religions.

Working in small groups, give your community a name. Then decide which four facilities are the most important for the community, to help people get on well. Say why you have chosen these four and then suggest one more that is not illustrated.

Would you add places of worship? Explain why.

Pub

Nursery

School

Shop

Youth club

Post office

Café

Town hall

Local councils can provide opportunities for people to mix, because only then will they understand each other and live together happily side by side.

Activity

1a) Look at the suggestions below and decide which ones you agree with.

b) Choose two which you consider to be the best or most important.

2 Can you think of any other solutions? Write your suggestions on sticky notes and display them on a board. Vote on the best suggestions.

Have a swimming pool and leisure centre that local people can afford to use.

Make sure that schools take their pupils from the different ethnic groups in an area so that there is a good mix in each school.

Provide a community centre or place where people can meet and hold events and entertainments, e.g. to celebrate religious festivals.

Set up a café where drinks and food are cheap and there are facilities for mothers with babies and toddlers.

Set up a youth shelter where young people can hang out without being hassled by police.

Encourage the setting up of groups, e.g. residents' committee on housing estate, to work with their councillors to sort out problems.

Library

Have a sports centre where there are a range of structured activities for young people.

Set up a committee for the area to arrange inter-cultural events where people from different groups can display their cultures.

Community centre

Have a range of small shops, e.g. grocer's, baker's, in the local area to serve people's needs and allow people to meet and talk to each other.

Cinema

Theatre

If we don't ever meet and get to know people who are different from us, but we nevertheless think we know what they are like, then we are basing our opinions on stereotypes.

Stereotypes are descriptions of groups of people based on what they have in common, such as their age, their religion, their race, their sex or their nationality. The description is applied to everyone in the group and ignores the individual differences between people.

So people might say:

- 'If they are old/young, they must be …'
- 'If they are Christian/Muslim, they must be …'
- 'If they are black/white, they must be …'
- 'If they're boys/girls, they must be …'
- 'If they are from country X, they must be …'

People may have something in common with others who share certain characteristics, but it does not mean that they all think or act in the same way.

---

1 Work in pairs. On a large sheet of paper, draw a stereotype of a young person today. Label the picture to show the kind of clothes you think they wear. Also show by labels or drawings this person's interests, tastes in music, etc.

2 Display the pictures around the room. Compare them. Put them into groups.

3 a) Do your pictures give an accurate image of young people today?
b) Are all young people like the ones in the pictures?
c) Where do stereotypes of young people come from?

You Englanders have won this time but I vill have my revenge!

A German soldier in the Second World War

4 Working in groups of four or five, look at the four pictures on these two pages.
a) Decide what each picture is suggesting about the group they represent.
b) How do illustrations like this make us think about certain groups of people?
c) Why do people use stereotypes like these in newspapers, comics, cartoons and magazines?

A football supporter

Pensioners

A single mother

5 a) What other stereotypes have you heard about?

b) Where have you heard or seen them?

c) Where do you think stereotypes come from?

d) Why do people believe them?

e) How do they affect the way people treat each other?

f) How might they affect the way you see yourself and what you do in the future?

Challenging stereotypes

Have you heard this story? A little boy was knocked down on his way to school. He was walking along, holding his father's hand, when a lorry hit him. He was rushed to hospital in an ambulance and taken straight to the operating theatre. The surgeon came in, gasped and exclaimed, 'That's my son!' What is the relationship of the surgeon to the boy?

*See the note below for the answer.

6 Write out the situations A–E and complete them in a way that challenges stereotypes, using one of the phrases 1–5 from the list on the right.

A Two lorry drivers were sitting in a transport café chatting about the jams on the motorway. On the way back to their lorries, one of the lorry drivers …

1 … lightweight wheelchair

B A group of Second World War veterans meet up every year to talk about their wartime experiences in …

2 … called her husband on her mobile phone

C A motor-bike rider was stopped by the police for speeding. The police officer noted his age, and said, …

3 … the Ghurkha Regiment

D The athlete who won the marathon was very fit. She also had the very latest …

4 … at the Hindu Temple

E The Member of Parliament was looking forward to his daughter's wedding, to be held …

5 … 'at 65 you should know better'.

7 Working in pairs, make up three more examples of your own, like the ones above.

*The surgeon was the boy's mother. This story challenges a stereotype of the kinds of work that women do.

Some of the most damaging stereotypes are racial stereotypes. We attach certain characteristics to people from a particular ethnic group or who come from a particular country. We all know about the image of Germans in the Second World War. We know that some people in European countries think that all young Englishmen are hooligans, yobs and lager louts.

These stereotypes are based on prejudice – opinions that people form without knowing all the facts. People often make up their minds quickly about other people without knowing much about them or taking the time to get to know them. Prejudices can be harmful when people are treated unfairly because of them. When people are treated unfairly because of prejudice about their race or colour, they are the victims of racial discrimination, and this is against the law.

Prejudice can lead to people calling others racist names, taunting them about the colour of their skin and making their lives uncomfortable. In the worst cases, it can lead to actual violent attacks. Read the following case study in which Maqsood Ahmad talks about his experiences of racism in Rochdale.

Maqsood

" My earliest memories of racism are from a school in Rochdale, where I grew up. I remember people not sitting next to me, throwing things and calling me names. There were only two or three Asians in my class. The teachers saw it as children playing pranks. It was a hostile environment for people like me. Even outside the school you couldn't really get away from it. My mother wouldn't let me play football outside; she wanted to protect me, but you end up excluded [cut off] from society.

[When I was older] I realised I couldn't get away from racism. You get your windows smashed, dog dirt through your letter box, your mother is spat at when she goes to the shops, your sister is sworn at and her headscarf is pulled off. It all made me very angry. Only the good sense of my mother and father made me see that not every white person is racist.

If you are attacked on a regular basis, you get worn down. Every time you meet someone you wonder, 'Are they treating me differently?' Even if they are not, you are suspicious because of your experience. If my parents hadn't kept talking to me about these issues, I think I'd have ended up hating white people; it's a common reaction.

Racist organisations were active in Rochdale when I was growing up. If no action is taken, they become more confident. But in areas where communities are strong, with good anti-racist activists and the police force taking strong action and rooting these individuals out, others don't express these views. "

Activity

1 Sometimes we see racism going on around us, but don't know what we can do to help prevent it. Look at the following chart in which some suggestions have been made. Discuss these suggestions in small groups and try to think of other ways in which people could have helped Maqsood.

Maqsood's experiences	What could have been done to help
People wouldn't sit next to him at school	Class sit alphabetically Discussions in class about why people from the Commonwealth were invited to come to the UK
Things thrown at him Maqsood called names Teachers saw it as children playing pranks	School policy on bullying Class discussion on bullying Maqsood gets support from his peers (people of around the same age)
Mother protected Maqsood and he felt excluded	Friends call round at his house and meet his family They invite him to play football with them
Racist organisations	Classmates and friends find out the facts about racist political parties, and the law that aims to protect minority ethnic groups

2 Sometimes people are racist in our presence. It is important, but difficult, to challenge these people. Working in pairs, write down how you would deal with the following situations:

A A member of your family makes a racist comment while you are watching a television programme.

B A friend points to someone in the street and calls out a racist name.

C A member of your class refuses to work in your group with someone because of their race or ethnic group.

D Someone at your youth club tells you a racist joke.

3 Discuss in class what different pairs have suggested for the above situations, and the problems involved in taking a stand.

Tackling racism

Tackling racist behaviour, whether it is bullying, racist violence or racial discrimination, is taken seriously by local councils, schools, the government and the police. It is not just something that individuals have to cope with alone. There are lots of examples of successful work tackling racism. Here is one.

Racism in sport

For many years, particularly in the 1970s and 1980s, black football players suffered abuse and racist chants at football matches. People from ethnic minorities did not go to football matches for fear they would be harassed and intimidated. Organisations like 'Let's Kick Racism Out of Football' and 'Show Racism the Red Card' were set up in the 1990s and are supported by football clubs and supporters' groups. Clubs agreed to a plan to challenge racism inside football stadiums. They put anti-racist statements in programmes, on posters and around the grounds. They made public address announcements condemning racist chants and they took action against fans and players who engaged in racist abuse.

The campaign has been very successful. Most black players say that the situation now is much better than it was, and people in this country are shocked when they hear of racism at international matches abroad. However, fans, referees and players are still racially abused, particularly at amateur level. Lots of clubs are working on their own anti-racist schemes with youth groups and schools in their local area.

Artwork produced by a young person as part of Show Racism the Red Card's annual schools competition. The organisation is an anti-racist charity which harnesses the high profile of professional sports people to educate young people about the dangers of racism

Activity

1 Find out more about the work of Kick It Out and Show Racism the Red Card from their websites: www.kickitout.org and www.theredcard.org.
2 Racism happens in many sports, not just football. Choose a sport and design, paint or draw your own anti-racist posters, postcards, T-shirts or badges. Or you could write a poem like Elljay's opposite. Think carefully about the message, and the best way of putting it across.

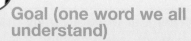

Goal (one word we all understand)

We all speak different languages
Some you can't understand
Some use broken English
Some sign with their hands
We got pattwa, slang, Creole and pidgin
You got accents from countries with bits of English missing
But travel the world and most places you go
When the ball hits the back of the net
Everybody shouts
GOAL!!!!

(Source: Elljay, Pitchprose.org, 2004)

What can schools do to prevent racism?

'Schools have a duty to eliminate unlawful racial discrimination and to promote equality of opportunity and good relations between people of different groups.' (Race Relations Amendment Act 2000).

Most schools have some kind of statement saying what they will do to try to encourage understanding between different groups, and also how they will deal with any instances of racist behaviour.

The law about race
- In the United Kingdom, the Race Relations Act of 1976 makes it illegal to discriminate against anyone because of their race, colour, nationality or ethnic origin. This applies to jobs, training, housing, education and the provision of goods and services.
- Racial violence is an offence under the criminal law. Inciting or encouraging racial hatred is also an offence under the criminal law. This means that if you are found guilty, you become a criminal and can be sent to prison.

Activity

1 One school suggested some ways to encourage racial equality and understanding. You can see these below. Work in pairs and decide:
   a) which suggestions you agree with
   b) which suggestions you partly agree with but want to change some of it or say 'it depends…'
   c) which ones you don't agree with or don't think are important
   d) if you would like to add anything.
2 Pairs join together in fours, share your thoughts on the suggestions and see if any of you change your minds.
3 Find out what your own school policy says on anti-racism. Discuss ways your policy could be improved and prepare a presentation on this to make to a senior member of staff.

A Links are made with schools in other parts of the country and other parts of the world.

B The school is open to all people of all groups who want to come to it.

C The content of lessons (what is taught) should reflect the different groups in the community, e.g. History, Art, Music, Religious Education, English, etc.

D Children's names are recorded accurately in registers and pronounced correctly.

E When choosing material for lessons, care should be taken to present positive images of minority ethnic groups and challenges to stereotypes.

F Assemblies use stories, poems, songs and dance from a variety of different cultures.

G The school provides a wide variety of visits and visitors to widen children's horizons.

Schools also have a duty to help pupils to understand different cultures and to encourage them to get along with each other in school. They should also encourage pupils to find out about the wider community outside the school, and about people who have different backgrounds.

Think about things that pupils in your school could do within your local community to help other people and to find out more about them.

Here are some suggestions.

Volunteering for a local environmental project

Singing in a community choir

Collecting for a charity

Taking part in a fun run for a good cause

Organising a petition

Participating in a local inter-cultural event

Activity

1 Which of these types of activities on pages 58–9 have you been involved in? Are there any not illustrated here that you have done?
2 What are the benefits of activities like these:
   a) for you
   b) for the community
   c) for the school?
3 What else should a school do to make closer links with people who live in the local community?
4 Plan a school linking project. With your teacher's help, choose a school in a different part of your town (or county). Someone in the class may already have a friend or relative in the school.

a) Once the link is agreed by the headteachers of both schools, write letters or emails to the pupils and include pictures of your class, your school and local area.
b) Describe all the interests of the pupils in your class.
c) Ask the pupils in the link school to send information about theirs and discuss the similarities and differences between the two communities.
d) You could follow this up with: a regular diary of 'life in our school', visits of pupils between schools, a joint exhibition or event, such as a debate on an issue affecting the whole area.

Reflection

How well do you think you're doing?
Think back over the work you've done in Section 2.

Skills

- Draw a chart like the one below, and give yourself a grade from 1 to 5, where 1 is the lowest and 5 is the highest.
- Give evidence for your score and say how you could improve your skills.

Assessing your progress
In this section you will be assessing how well you can:

- discuss different ideas, opinions and beliefs
- take account of other people's views
- explain your own opinion and give reasons for it
- plan some action with other people
- understand the issues to do with living in communities, including differences between groups of people.

How well can you ... ?	1	2	3	4	5	Evidence for your score?	How can you improve?
discuss different ideas							
explain your opinions							
listen to and take other people's opinions into account							
plan some action							

Understanding

- How are councils elected?
- Why are local councils important to people's lives and why should we know about how they work?
- Choose one of these images and say why it is a stereotype. Why can stereotypes be dangerous?

- What are the reasons for people not getting on in communities?
- What can be done to help people get along better?
- Talk to another pupil and discuss what you think was the most important thing you learned in this section.

Section 3

Human rights in a global community

We all know a lot more about what goes on in other countries than people used to. Modern technology, such as satellite phones and the internet, as well as easy air travel, helps people in different countries to communicate all the time. Because of all this communication, we know when governments are treating their people well and when they are not. Most countries in the world have signed up to the United Nations Declaration of Human Rights, which is supposed to protect people from discrimination and oppression. However, there are still many problems in the world. People are sometimes so badly treated that they have to flee to safety somewhere else. And sometimes people choose to live in another country because they want a better life. People move around the world much more than they used to.

What abuses of rights do some people suffer, and what can be done to help?

What are human rights and why do they need to be protected?

Why do people choose to move to another country to live?

How much freedom should the press have to report on issues of concern?

Assessing your progress
In this section you will:

- examine different sources of information
- debate your views with other people
- develop your campaigning skills
- practise your presentation skills
- think about ways of solving global problems
- develop your understanding of human rights and responsibilities.

KEY WORDS

human rights

people trafficking

slavery

migration

press freedom

Citizens of Planet Hoff

You are part of a team visiting Planet Hoff to compare their society with that on Earth. You have already met some of the inhabitants of Planet Hoff in Book 1 of this series.

There are five groups of citizens on Hoff. They are born into one of the groups. Very few citizens manage to move into different groups.

Uppers rule Hoff. They are very rich and live in grand houses. Although there are only a few of them, they tell all the other citizens what to do.

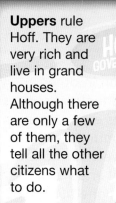

Thinkers help to run the government of Hoff, carrying out the orders of the Uppers. They run the television stations and do jobs such as doctors, lawyers and teachers. Some Thinkers don't think that the Uppers should make all the decisions; they want to have a say in how Hoff is run. When they organised meetings to protest, their leaders were arrested and the Uppers passed a law banning such meetings.

Activity

1 What do you think is unfair about the way things are run on Hoff?
2 Recommend some changes that would improve the lives of all its citizens.
3 List five 'rights' that you think all citizens on Hoff should have.
4 Name two things that you would find completely unacceptable on Earth.

Capitos run the factories and farms on Hoff. They sell goods that they make, both on Hoff and to other planets. Hoff is famous for its crystal clocks and space travel technology. Some Capitos would like to do the jobs the Thinkers do, but the high schools are only open to the children of Thinkers. Every year a few Capito children are selected by exam to go to a high school. Most Capito children go to the low schools that teach a limited number of subjects.

Doers work in factories or on farms. Their wages are fixed at a low level by the Uppers, and they all have to work long hours every week. However, they are guaranteed a home to live in, and the price of basic foods is fixed. The Doers are not allowed to travel to other parts of Hoff unless they get special permission. The Doers are not allowed to go to schools. They are given a certain job and trained in how to do it.

Gronks are at the bottom of society. They are not free. They are owned by Uppers or Thinkers, and do all the domestic jobs, like cooking and cleaning in the homes of their owners. They have electronic implants in their heads that allow their owners to control them. If they have children, the children become the property of the owner. The Gronks can be bought and sold. They have their own religion, but they are not allowed to worship their gods. They are severely beaten if caught doing so.

Can you say what you think on Hoff?

The Thinkers broadcast television programmes and write the daily electronic news sheets. In the past, the writers of news sheets that criticised the Uppers were put in prison. Now the Uppers censor all television programmes and news sheets before they go out. Articles and programmes:

- must not criticise the Uppers or government
- cannot suggest changes to the way of life on Hoff
- must never use swear words or offensive images
- should make the inhabitants feel good about their lives, so they are not allowed to show any bad aspects of Hoff.

Anybody who speaks out against the Uppers and the government is arrested and punished.

Can you get justice on Hoff?

The police on Hoff are under the direct control of the Uppers and the government. The Uppers make the laws that everybody has to obey. The police carry out the instructions of the rulers.

If someone is arrested they are brought to court. There is one judge, an Upper, who listens to the evidence and then decides whether the offender is guilty or not. There are no juries. The Doers and the Gronks cannot have lawyers to represent them and are not allowed to put their side of a case. For them, the judge listens to what the police and witnesses say and then decides if they are guilty.

3.2 What are human rights?

Human rights are basic rights that everyone is entitled to and that all human beings should expect to have, such as the right to life and freedom from slavery.

The idea of human rights has developed through history in different societies. There are some important points in this development:

Magna Carta, 1215

A document signed in England by King John. From this came the ideas that people should not be arrested without having a fair trial and that rulers should seek the consent of people before laws are passed.

Activity

Divide the class up so that different groups are looking at one of the four key human rights documents on this page. Each has to research their document and come back to the class to tell them:

• how it came to be written
• what was going on at the time
• other interesting information about it.

The American Declaration of Independence, 1776

When America became an independent country, the Founding Fathers set out in the declaration the key ideas or principles upon which it would be governed, and the rights that American citizens had. It started with these famous words:

'We hold these truths to be self-evident, that all men are created equal, that they are endowed by their Creator with certain unalienable rights, that amongst these are life, liberty and the pursuit of happiness.'

The Declaration of the Rights of Man, 1789

When the French overthrew their king in the French Revolution they also wrote a document setting out the key rights of citizens. Some of the main ones are:

• men are born free and equal in rights
• liberty to do what you want as long as you don't harm others
• free speech – able to talk and write freely
• can own property
• laws should be made with the agreement of the people.

The United Nations Declaration of Human Rights, 1948

After the horrors of two world wars the people from countries all over the world came together to form the United Nations (UN). They decided that they needed a statement of human rights for all of the people in the world and produced the Universal Declaration of Human Rights. It was approved by the UN on 10 December 1948. This document was meant to be a standard by which people could judge whether a government was treating its people properly. Nearly all the countries of the world have signed it.

Here is a summary of some of the rights set out in the UN declaration.

1 All human beings are born free and equal in dignity and rights.

2 Everyone is entitled to all the rights and freedoms in this declaration without distinction of any kind, such as race, colour, sex, language, political or other opinion, national or social origin, property, birth or other status.

3 Everyone has the right to life and liberty.

4 No one shall be held in slavery.

5 No one shall be subjected to torture or to cruel, inhuman or degrading treatment or punishment.

6 All are equal before the law.

7 No one shall be subjected to arbitrary (unreasonable) arrest, detention or exile.

8 Everyone is entitled to a fair trial, in public.

9 Everyone accused of a crime in a court of law is presumed innocent until proved guilty in a public trial in which they have a right to defend themselves.

10 No one shall be subjected to interference with their privacy, family, home or correspondence.

11 Everyone has the right of freedom of movement and residence within the borders of each state, and the right to leave and return freely to their country.

12 Everyone has the right to seek asylum from persecution in other countries.

13 Men and women of full age have the right to marry and found a family without limitation due to race, nationality or religion.

14 Everyone has the right to own property.

15 Everyone has the right to freedom of thought, conscience and religion.

16 Everyone has the right to freedom of opinion and expression.

17 Everyone has the right to meet freely in peaceful organisations.

18 Everyone has the right to take part in the government of their country.

19 Everyone has the right to work, to free choice of employment, and to equal pay for equal work.

20 Everyone has the right to rest and leisure.

21 Everyone has the right to a standard of living adequate for the health and well-being of themselves and their family, including food, clothing, housing and medical care.

22 Everyone has the right to an education. Education shall be free and compulsory.

23 Everyone has the right to take part in the cultural life of the community.

DISCUSS

On pages 66–7 you will read some case studies that show why we need a strong declaration of human rights. Why do you think some countries are not keen to give all their citizens these rights?

Why do we need to protect human rights?

Activity

Each of the case studies on pages 66–7 represents different aspects of the abuse of human rights. On a copy of the chart below, for each one:

1 Note down some key facts about them.
2 Using the summary on page 65, explain what rights are being denied to the people involved.

Type of human rights abuse	What rights are being abused (list articles from the UN Declaration of Rights being broken)
Forced labour – people forced to work for little or no money. Often trapped.	

A Bonded labour

People borrow money or get into debt. To repay it they become a bonded labourer. But the interest on the money is so high and the pay they receive so low that they never pay off the debt. This can last for the whole of their lives and even be passed on to their children. It happens most commonly in India and Brazil. Leelu Bai was a bonded labourer in India:

" I became bonded after I got married twenty years ago. My husband's family has been bonded for three generations to the same landlord. They took loans for marriage, for illness, for education and so it went on ... I used to work from 6a.m. in the landlord's house, cleaning and fetching water. Then I would go to work on the farm ... until 7p.m. or later. "

(Source: adapted from www.antislavery.org)

B Freedom of speech

Chinese human rights activist Hu Jia was sentenced to three and a half years in prison in March 2008 in Beijing for speaking out against China's human rights violations. Hu was denied access to his lawyer, members of his family and medical treatment, including necessary daily medication for liver disease. Due to his activities and outspokenness, Hu Jia was repeatedly harassed and beaten by police, particularly in the run-up towards the 2008 Olympic Games. He has been imprisoned on several occasions, adding up to over four years in total.

C Forced labour

In Brazil, men who are poor are lured to work on farms deep in the rainforest and are used as forced labour to clear land. Once they get to the farms they find they are paid very little and most of that is taken by the 'gato' or gang master for food and accommodation. They live in shacks and are trapped because they have no money to get home or there are armed guards who threaten them. Raimundo, 27, was offered a good wage. But when he got to the farm, the farmer said he would pay them less and would take money out of their wages for food and tools. Raimundo says:

> *This way we were not able to make any money. I was thinking about my family. At home they desperately needed money.*

Being so far from home, he needed to work to earn some money but it was hard and there was no reward. So he decided to escape. Men who tried to escape had been captured and beaten, but Raimundo, without money or food, managed to walk and hitch lifts till he got home.

(Adapted from material produced by Anti-Slavery International.)

D Sex slavery

Sabina was only twelve years old when she was lured from her home in Bangladesh and ended up in a brothel in India. Sabina's family were very poor, and she and her mother went from house to house cleaning in exchange for food. Like so many other girls, she was lured by promises of a good job and better pay by an older Indian woman. Sabina could not read and write and so did not know where she was being taken. She was sold to a brothel where she was then repeatedly used by up to fifteen men a night. She was beaten and tortured till she did what they wanted. She was also forced to do all the housework during the day. Eventually she managed to escape and returned home. But she was not welcomed as a shamed woman, was called names, and was not allowed to share in the life of the village.

(Adapted from a case study from the Church Mission Society, who helped Sabina to find a job, some education and a more pleasant life.)

Modern slavery

It is thought that between 12 and 20 million people are at this moment in some form of slavery around the world. It is very difficult to know exact numbers because by its nature much of this exploitation is secret and hidden away. It is mostly found in poor Asian, African and Latin American countries, but it can be found in developed countries and it does exist in the UK.

Modern slavery takes many different forms such as forced labour, domestic slavery, sex slavery and bonded labour. You have seen some examples of these on pages 66–67.

Human trafficking

Human trafficking is when people are tricked or forced to leave their homes and move to another place or country where they are exploited in slave-like work. Usually they cannot move around freely and receive very little pay. They are controlled by threats or violence. You have read the case of Sabina (page 67). The United Nations estimates that over 1.5 million children are trafficked worldwide each year and possibly 2 million adults.

Trafficking is global and Europe is not excluded. Hundreds of thousands of people from Africa, Asia and China have been trafficked into Europe and the UK to work in domestic slavery, agricultural work, the food industry or construction. Many children and young women from Eastern Europe are trafficked into the sex trade and prostitution – around 4000 at any one time according to UK government estimates. They are often held captive by threats to their families at home.

> **Why does slavery still exist?** How can there be so much slavery today, when it is against international law and illegal in most countries? The main reason is poverty. In many parts of the world there are huge numbers of people, especially on the outskirts of cities, who have no jobs and are poor, hungry and desperate. It is easy to exploit these people and use them. Governments lack the will or the forces to stop it.
>
> The other main reason is that some people can make a lot of money by dealing in slaves and bringing cheap labour to mining, agriculture, building works or prostitution. This leads to corruption, with government officials taking bribes to turn a blind eye.

Activity

Work in small groups. Your task is to make other people more aware of modern slavery. You can focus on one form, for example bonded labour, or choose several different areas. Choose one of the following formats:

- a presentation
- a radio programme
- a leaflet or poster.

Use the information on this page but do some further research. There is a great deal of information on the internet. You will find the websites listed on page 69 useful.

An Ethiopian domestic worker hanging washed clothes in Lebanon

DISCUSS

Why do you think the people in case studies A, C and D on pages 66–7 were pulled into slavery?

Developing your campaigning skills

Activity

You've collected the information to tell people about slavery and trafficking. Your next task is to plan a campaign to tell more people about what is going on and persuade them to join the fight against modern slavery. Think about the following:

- Who are you going to target the campaign on?
- How will you raise money to pay for the campaign?
- How will you get people interested so that they support you?

Draw up a plan of what you are going to do. Look at the Tactics below that show different ways you could campaign.

Choose the ones that would be best for your project (don't pick too many). You can get some ideas by looking at the websites mentioned below. Present your campaign ideas to the rest of the class. You could run an awareness campaign in your school.

Websites
www.antislavery.org
www.cms-uk.org
www.iabolish.org
www.hrw.org/campaigns
www.notforsalecampaign.org
www.ethicaltrade.org

Tactic

Draw up petitions that people can sign.

Tactic

Hold music concerts or special events to get funds to support the campaign and increase public awareness.

Tactic

Encourage people to support products made through fair trade or ethical trading schemes (see the Ethical Trading website listed).

Tactic

Put pressure on companies that use child or slave labour to produce their products. Perhaps you could hold a demonstration.

Tactic

Get newspapers or television interested so that they make people aware of your campaign.

Tactic

Get powerful people or celebrities to support your campaign.

Tactic

Hold debates and meetings to make people aware of the issue.

Tactic

Write letters to Members of Parliament.

Tactic

Hold fundraising events or plan schemes to support people who have escaped.

Tactic

Boycott goods produced by child or slave labour.

3.3 It's a global world!

If we look back into our own histories, we can usually find members of our family who have made a decision to leave their birthplace and seek a better life in another country. People have come to the United Kingdom over centuries to make up the rich and varied population we have today. Similarly, many people have left the UK to go and live in other countries, such as Australia, Canada and parts of Africa. Hundreds of thousands of people are leaving the UK every year.

People migrate for many reasons. Usually these reasons are to do with:

- things that cause people to leave their homeland – push factors
- things that attract people to new countries – pull factors.

People do not usually move for just one reason. The decision to migrate is taken for a variety of 'push' and 'pull' reasons.

Activity

1 Decide which of the factors below are 'push' factors, and which are 'pull' factors. Complete your own copy of the following chart.

Push	Pull

- **a)** High unemployment
- **b)** People needed to do jobs
- **c)** Civil war
- **d)** Better education
- **e)** People can say what they like without fear of imprisonment
- **f)** Fear of being persecuted because of religion
- **g)** Fear of imprisonment and torture because of political views
- **h)** Hunger
- **i)** Better paid jobs
- **j)** Safety, strong system of law and order
- **k)** Enough food and water for everybody
- **l)** Better housing
- **m)** Fear of attack because of ethnic group
- **n)** Poverty, little chance to make a good living
- **o)** Overcrowding, not enough land to go around
- **p)** War with a neighbouring country
- **q)** Freedom of expression and movement

2 Match speech bubbles A–H below with one of the push/pull factors in your chart from question 1. For example, B matches c) Civil war.

A I had heard that the government of this country wanted people to come and work in certain jobs, as there were not enough people to do them.

B There has been a war going on in my country for ten years. Nobody is safe and there is no chance of building a decent life for my family.

C I was forced to join the army at the age of thirteen to fight for our country. I am now fourteen and I am frightened that I am going to be killed.

D I was against the government and said so in public. I was beaten and threatened that I would be tortured or killed if I spoke out again.

E Our relatives say the country is very wealthy and, if you work hard, you can be successful.

F In this country you are free to say what you like and go where you like.

G The soldiers beat me and my daughters because of our religion. We couldn't bear it any more.

H I am a trained doctor but there are no jobs here. I want to live somewhere where I could work and earn a better living for my family.

The United Kingdom is a member of the European Union (EU), along with 26 other countries. Countries from central and eastern Europe have joined in the last few years and others are waiting to join.

The European Union was set up after the end of the Second World War, to improve trade between its original six members and to try to make sure that the countries of Europe would never fight each other again. The EU set up the 'common market'. This means that all goods, services and people in the EU can travel freely in its area. The advantage to the member countries is a better standard of living for their people, although there is still a lot of disagreement about some of the rules.

Map showing EU member states

All citizens of an EU country have the right to live and work in any of the other countries. People from central and eastern Europe (from Poland, Bulgaria or Slovakia, for example) have a legal right to be here. People who are citizens of Britain also have the right to live and work in any other country of the EU. The countries that have been members for the longest often have the strongest economies, and some people decide to move temporarily for work. In the 1980s Germany had a much stronger economy than Britain, and many young people, especially builders, did exactly this.

Auf Wiedersehen, Pet

A television comedy, called *Auf Wiedersehen, Pet* ran between1983 and 2004. In the first series, it followed three bricklayers – Dennis, Neville and Oz – from Newcastle upon Tyne who set off for Germany, leaving their families behind, in an attempt to find work, make some money and to have some adventures. When the series was devised, there were 30,000 workers from the north east of England working in Germany because they couldn't find work at home. The three bricklayers got work in the German district of Düsseldorf, where they met up and shared a hut with other building workers from across Britain.

In the first episode, Neville is missing his wife and finding the work difficult. He injures his hand while pretending to be a skilled carpenter, and Oz teases him about his work getting even slower than the German workers and not being able to write postcards home.

Activity

1 Read the extract from the script and decide why Oz, Neville, Barry and their friends decided to go to Germany to work.
2 Discuss the hardships they might have faced and the disadvantages of leaving family to work abroad.

NEVILLE:	I'm not here because I like it, Oz. Some of us, like me and Dennis, we're only going through with this because we've got a purpose.
OZ:	I thought you had a whale, not a porpoise! What do you feed that on?
DENNIS:	Oz, you never know when to leave it alone, do you?
NEVILLE:	You're the one that's out of step, Oz. What's so comical about me writing to my wife? What's so strange about me caring for her, worrying about her? Dennis is the same with his missus. You're just doing this for her, aren't you Den? And the bairns.

LATER ON THEY COLLECT THEIR FIRST PAY PACKET.

DENNIS:	There you go, Nev. That makes it all worthwhile, your first pay packet.
BOMBER:	And Bomber's last!
SITE MANAGER:	What? You are leaving?
BOMBER:	And not soon enough, my old duck. Got a nice job lined up, I have – Bristol, new bypass. Good money, home every night, and English ale!

European migrants in Britain

In recent years the European Union has 'enlarged' because new countries from East and Central Europe such as Poland, Hungary and Lithuania have joined. Many people from these countries looked to Western Europe for a new life, for work and to make some money, and some of them came to Britain.

At first a lot of people came, and then, after a few years, some went home. There were many stories in the newspapers about the numbers coming here and the kind of work they were doing. Here is one story about Bartek and Natalia, living in Glasgow.

Sitting outside the Polish café run by his parents in the west end of Glasgow, is 21-year-old Bartek Korzeniowski and his friend Natalia Tomkowiak. They both grew up in the same city in Poland, but only really got to know each other at Glasgow University, where they are students. Both came here a few years ago for one reason: education.

Korzeniowski's view on Scotland sums up how many young Poles view immigration and multiculturalism: 'Is Britain my home? No. The point of the new immigration is that it is very fluid. It is not difficult to get a flight tomorrow and go somewhere else to start your life. Twenty years ago, people were stuck in one place and had to spend all their lives there. We're European citizens. We aren't just moving here to get more money or better jobs, it's also because we are in the European Union and quite simply can move around if we want to.'

He admits money is a factor for many young Poles moving to the UK, but it doesn't appear to have been the main reason for his family. His mother and father both held down good jobs in banking and the restaurant trade. They moved to Britain as they wanted a life change.

Unlike African or Asian immigrants, Poles have not suffered the extremes of British racism, aside from a few violent and unpleasant incidents. 'All in all, Scottish people have been very friendly,' he adds. 'Some people have had negative experiences – maybe a racist remark when someone is drunk. Others have been given the worst jobs at work – but I believe that is usually because they have poor skills with the English language. If you can't speak English you tend to end up categorised as a second-class citizen.'

Natalia Tomkowiak's experience was a little harder. She worked as a waitress, barmaid and cleaner before finally getting her latest student job – as a translator. Her first summer here saw her working 50-hour weeks to make enough money to pay her way through university … She's now trying to set up the Polish Arts and Cultural Association in Glasgow to bring Scottish and Polish people together.

The young students stress there is no such thing as a 'representative' Pole – and they have learned that there is no such thing as a 'representative' Brit. 'I came here for self development, as well as to work,' says Tomkowiak. 'I would never have sung in a rock band back home, here I did it. To move to another country is such a boost to your life. And I have never been lonely. The Scots have been wonderful and friendly. These have been the best two years of my life.'

Adapted from The New Scots: Immigrants' Stories, by Neil Mackay, *The Sunday Herald*, Aug 27, 2006

Newspapers and European migration

Newspapers do not always give the same picture of migration. Some emphasise the large numbers coming here, and suggest that these people cause problems of one sort or another. Other papers give a more positive view and report on the advantages of migration for our economy.

On this page are some of the words and phrases that have been used by British newspapers when they report on European migration.

Big influx of Eastern European immigrants to the UK

Immigration is placing huge strain on Britain

Migrant crime wave a myth

Schools struggling to cope with migrant children

Migrants are a boon to UK economy

Eastern European migrants going home

Migrants are reliable workers, say employers

Eastern European immigrants carry out a tenth of crime

British workers lack skills and drive of east Europe's migrants, says study

Activity

1 Which of these headlines on this page is positive, and which is negative about European migration? Are any of them neutral?
2 Look at the words used in each headline and decide which words are trying to persuade the reader to think in a particular way.
3 What issues are raised about migration in these headlines?
4 Find examples of newspaper articles that report on migration. Decide whether the article is positive, negative or neutral about migration, and decide which words led you to that conclusion. Research European migration and write a neutral article about it.

DISCUSS

1 What does Bartek feel are the advantages of European citizens being able to move around Europe easily? Do you agree with his views?
2 Why did Bartek and Natalia come to Scotland and what were their experiences of living and working there?
3 How is this newspaper representing the 'new' immigrants?

3.5 Refugees

Throughout history, families have been forced to flee their homes because they have been victimised and made to fear for their lives. The Pilgrim Fathers fled to America in the seventeenth century to escape persecution. In the nineteenth century, Jews were forced to flee from Russia and Eastern Europe because their homes were being attacked. In the twentieth century, two world wars led to millions of people being left without a home as they were pushed out of land they had once lived in.

After the Second World War, the United Nations (UN) was determined to do something about the plight of refugees. It set up the United Nations High Commission on Refugees (UNHCR), which encourages countries to work together to try to protect the rights of refugees. The aim is to help them to return to their own country or, if they are still threatened, to settle somewhere else.

Alfager refugee camp in Pakistan-administered Kashmir

The refugee problem has not improved in recent years. Civil wars, brutal governments and fighting between different ethnic groups have led to the same old story of violence and persecution, causing people to leave their homes. There are millions of refugees living in developing countries that are themselves poor. A few find refuge in richer countries, where they settle into new lives with homes and jobs.

As part of the UN Convention, people fleeing oppression have the right to claim asylum (safety) in countries that have signed up to the convention.

Displaced members of the Luo tribe queue for food at a refugee camp near Limuru west of Nairobi, Kenya

People tend to think of refugees as large groups of people, but they are all individuals with their own stories to tell. The following stories come from young people who had to leave home.

Activity

1 Read the case studies of Jacob, Feah and Teshk on pages 77–8. Draw up a chart like the one below and answer the questions in note form.

	Jacob	Feah	Teshk
Where do they come from?			
Why were they forced to flee?			
What difficulties and dangers did they face on their journeys to safety?			

2 How does this change your idea of what a refugee is? Why would it be difficult for refugees to return quickly to their countries?

3 What other reasons (push factors) might force people to become refugees?

Jacob's story

" *In my home town, in the southern Sudan, there was fighting everywhere. Everyone was running from the bombs. Even our goats were bombed. No one had time to plant the crops. So I just left. There were so many people walking on the road. I had nothing. No clothes. No food. The first day I didn't eat. I just ran. The first night I remembered the wild animals I had seen along the road. I was afraid, so I climbed up a tree to sleep. But I couldn't sleep. I thought that something would come and pull me down.* "

Jacob joined up with many others on the road.

" *We walked and walked. We saw villages where there was nobody, not even a cat. We had no food, and people started eating leaves. After ten days people in our group began to die. One night an old man said he could not walk any more. An hour later he died. We crossed a river and planes dropped bombs on us. I was very tired but we reached the [refugee] camp in Ethiopia. There are many people here from Sudan just like me. Now I go to school again. In the camp there is food and medicine. The sound of planes no longer frightens me because I know they are carrying food not bombs. This is the place I dreamed of.* "

(Source: Adapted from *Refugee Children*, Geneva, UNHCR)

Painting by David Kumcieng, aged 15, Sudanese, Kakuma refugee camp.

'We wanted people to run, but we had to walk because we were tired and so hot and hungry. In my picture the people are wearing clothes, but of course we didn't have any clothes. We saw people dying, it was always the young ones, the hungry ones and the old ones.'

Feah's story

Feah is from Sierra Leone. Her normal, happy family life was shattered on the day that armed rebel soldiers suddenly arrived at her parents' cocoa plantation. Feah and the younger children of her family were collecting water from a nearby stream when they saw the rebels approach the plantation. Terrified, the children hid from the armed men, but from their hiding place they heard their mother's agonised cries as she was tortured by the soldiers.

The children could only stay where they were, hoping the vicious soldiers would go away without discovering them. When it was safe to leave their hiding place, the children found their mother, but she was dead. Feah and her brothers and sister searched for their father but could find no trace of him. Feah, the eldest child, now had to take her young brothers and her sister somewhere safe. As the children travelled on foot through the countryside, they avoided soldiers and others who might hurt them. The journey to safety took them seven days and seven nights. At the end, they reached the neighbouring country of Guinea, and sought shelter and safety in a refugee camp. Feah has had to grow up quickly. Her childhood ended abruptly the day her mother died.

At the age of fourteen, she was responsible for her four-year-old sister Kadiatu, and her brothers Aiah, ten, and Junior, aged two. A third brother, Komba, escaped with them; but during the flight from danger Komba caught a chill that developed into pneumonia. He died in Feah's arms. He was only five years old.

(Source: Adapted from *Refugee Teenagers – escape and protection from persecution and war*, UNHCR, 2001)

Teshk's story

Teshk is Kurdish and from Iraq. He and his family escaped to England when the family came to the notice of the Saddam Hussein government, before the war in Iraq.

❝ *We came under threat from Saddam Hussein's government. It was a very difficult time. I was expelled from school, although I was doing very well and had aimed to get a place in medical school. We had people coming to the house all the time asking questions. They were secret police. They would say, 'We are from the Ba'ath Party in your area and we would like to ask you a few questions.' If you were from a Kurdish background there was already a question mark over you, but because our uncle was in trouble there was another question mark. We were hassled on a daily basis. We expected my father to be arrested at any time, even though he was not involved in politics, but he could have been put in prison for any reason. We had to give up everything for our safety. We had to leave secretly, not tell the neighbours. We took just a small rucksack each and travelled on buses through Turkey and finally got to the UK from Istanbul. We had to smuggle money out of Iraq in the lining of a jacket to pay for the journey.* **❞**

(Source: *We All Came Here from Somewhere – diversity, identities and citizenship*, LSN/QIA, 2006)

How are refugees treated?

Nearly 10 million people in the world today are classified as refugees by the United Nations. The largest groups have escaped from Afghanistan, Burma, Somalia, Zimbabwe and Iraq. Three-quarters of all refugees settle in neighbouring poor countries, often in refugee camps. A few refugees manage to escape to richer countries. The Western countries that take most refugees are Germany and the USA.

Before a person is classified as a refugee, they have to 'claim asylum' (safety). This means that they have to prove to the country they have fled to that they have escaped from real danger and that they need to be somewhere safe. The decision is usually based on an interview at which the person claiming asylum has to provide evidence of the danger.

Whether the host country is rich or poor, refugees do not always receive a warm welcome, despite their often terrible experiences. Some people do not believe their stories and call them 'bogus asylum seekers'. Others think they are a drain on welfare services, or that refugees are taking jobs and housing.

Here are some comments made by young refugees about their experiences in Britain:

> First of all they put us in very high buildings surrounded by poor and homeless people. They look on us as a refugee. A lot of boys and girls say, 'Go home, refugee.' I'm a university lecturer in Iraq. This is not right.

Male, 27

> Before? What had we before? We could be in graves like the others back home. Now we have to prove ourselves, to show we are studying well, working well.

Male, 23

> We arrived in London, Victoria. We stayed in a bed and breakfast for two days – they charged us £860 for two days' stay. Of course, they knew we did not know what the currency was in this [country] – we were taken in.

Female, 18

> I'm back at school now – you have such a good standard of education here in the UK. You have a choice. I want to be creative, maybe an artist. I have no mind at all of being a housewife. I'd like to be a career lady.

Female, 16

> If you go to work, 'You're taking our jobs.' If you stay at home, they say, 'You're taking our money!'

Male, 16

(Source: *Starting Over – young refugees talk about life in Britain*, The Prince's Trust/The Diana, Princess of Wales Memorial Fund, 2002)

DISCUSS

1 What do the quotes above tell you about the problems young refugees have when they arrive in the UK?

2 What could be done to improve the situation? Consider: work, language, initial reception, money and food, education, somewhere to live.

Many people say that they prefer to live in countries where there is freedom to say or write what you think. Many countries that deny basic human rights also deny people this freedom. People who speak out or write in newspapers criticising the government of their country can be arrested and imprisoned.

In this country, we say that we have press freedom, but people disagree about whether newspapers have too much or not enough freedom.

Activity

The pictures on pages 80–1 show different points of view about press freedom. Match each picture with one of the statements below.

A

B

It's all lies! I'm ruined!

C

Statements

1 Newspapers dig into people's private lives and print things that cause a lot of damage.

2 We need newspapers to find out the truth, otherwise rich and powerful people could get away with wrongdoing.

3 The people have a right to know about matters that affect everyone.

4 Newspapers exaggerate or even tell lies to sell copies. They don't care if what they say is not true.

5 Famous people should expect others to be interested in their private lives. It's the price you pay for fame and fortune.

6 Newspaper journalists hound people to get stories.

7 The laws of libel in this country are strong enough to protect people. You can always sue in court.

8 Sometimes newspapers can affect the outcome of a trial because they print information that could influence a jury.

D

E

F

G

1 Which of the statements on page 80 argue *for* press freedom?
2 Which ones argue for more control of the press?
3 Which statements do you agree with?

H

If people feel that the press has behaved badly, they can complain to the Press Complaints Commission (PCC). This organisation was set up to keep an eye on the press and to decide when the press has broken its Code of Practice. The PCC uses the headings shown on page 84 to decide whether each complaint is justified.

Activity

You and a partner are the editors of a newspaper. You know that your readers are interested in politicians and celebrities. The following stories and photographs have been collected by journalists. Should you publish or not?

1 Consult the PCC Code of Practice on page 84 and decide whether each story breaks the code – and whether you would publish anyway.
2 Make up one or two cases of your own (or use news stories you have heard about) to give to other pairs or to discuss in class.

A well-known football player has been involved in a drunken brawl in a nightclub. The fight was over a girl whom the footballer has been seeing. However, he is married with children and does not want the story to be made public. Your reporter has collected interviews from people who know the footballer and she wants to get photographs of the footballer with his family outside his house. The footballer is angry. He says it is his private life and has nothing to do with anybody else. He says he is going to complain to the Press Council.

A celebrity has agreed that a well-known magazine can take and publish photographs of her wedding. No photographs are allowed to be taken by other newspapers or magazines. However, one of your newspaper photographers has managed to take some photographs secretly by pretending to be one of the caterers. One of your reporters also managed to interview guests by pretending to be from the rival magazine.

A woman has claimed that a famous politician told her secrets while they were having an affair. The politician denies knowing her. A photographer has photographs of the pair together. He took the pictures using a long-lens camera.

The maid of a member of the royal family has a very interesting story to tell about a relationship between the royal and a film star. She says she has also got evidence of the drunken activities of two young princesses, one of whom is under sixteen. There is even some talk that they may have been taking drugs. The maid wants a lot of money for the stories.

Royal maid reveals secret — EXCLUSIVE

Press Code of Practice

Accuracy – reports should be accurate and an apology must be published later if not

Opportunity to reply – people must be able to reply to inaccuracies

Privacy – people have a right to privacy and the use of long-lens photography is not allowed

Harassment – journalists and photographers must not continue to telephone or question after being asked to leave

Intrusion into grief or shock – enquiries must be sensitive when people are shocked or grieving

Children – children under the age of sixteen should not be photographed or interviewed on subjects involving their welfare without an adult present. They should not be approached at school. Children involved in sex cases should not be identified

Reporting of crime – relatives and friends of people convicted should not be identified, especially children

Victims of sexual assault – victims must not be identified unless there is justification

Misrepresentation – journalists cannot use trickery (for example, pretending to be somebody else) to get a story unless this can be justified in the public interest

Discrimination – journalists must not use a person's race, colour, religion, sex, sexual orientation or disability to describe them unless directly relevant to the story

Payment for articles – payment must not be made to witnesses in a court case or to convicted criminals for a story

Listening devices – no listening devices can be used

Hospitals – journalists and photographers must make themselves known to the authorities before entering public areas

Financial journalism – journalists must not use any information for their own gain

Confidential sources – journalists must respect confidential sources of information

Activity

Bring into class some celebrity magazines such as *Hello!* and *OK!*, and some music magazines.

1 Working in pairs or small groups, look at the way celebrities are shown in the magazines.
2 Discuss the complaints that celebrities may have when their images are used in this way. Think about:
   a) intrusions into their privacy
   b) being pestered in the street by people who think they know them
   c) stalkers.

In the 'public interest'?

People have a right to privacy, but sometimes there is a public interest in revealing what people do in private.

The problem is that it can be very difficult to decide exactly what 'public interest' means. It does not simply mean that the public are interested. The public – the readers of newspapers and watchers of television – are interested in most things about people, particularly their relationships and their sex lives.

'Public interest' is when it is important to know something about someone because they are public figures, funded out of taxpayers' money, or because what they do affects other people. For instance, if a member of the government accepts money or holidays from a rich businessman and then helps the man win a government building contract worth £2 million, then we should know. If a surgeon is taking drugs and attending wild parties while people are dying under her care, then we should know.

But how far should the press go? When do we have the right to know about the private life of a politician or celebrity, if at all?

> **DISCUSS**
>
> 1 Which of the stories below are in the 'public interest'?
> 2 Think back over the last few pages (80–5). Hold a class debate on whether you think the press should be more controlled or have more freedom.

A television presenter is shown in photographs to have put on a lot of weight. Newspapers show her with captions such as 'Presenter fills screen'.

A famous actress is photographed sunbathing topless on a Caribbean island.

A Member of Parliament is said to be receiving money from a wealthy foreign businessman to help him get a British passport.

A senior member of the government is divorcing his wife. She is very bitter and wants to tell her story to the newspapers and television shows.

A large tobacco company has been accused of targeting young people in African countries to try to encourage them to smoke cigarettes.

3.8 Speaking out!

In some countries there is little or no freedom of the press. Journalists are often put into prison, or even killed, for reporting anything that is critical of the government or other public figures. These days even writing an email or a blog on the internet can lead to arrest.

SUBRAMANIYAM SUGIRDHARAJAN: SRI LANKA

Journalist Subramaniyam Sugirdharajan was shot by unidentified men riding motorcycles after he had published photographs and news reports critical of the army in Sri Lanka.

AMIR ABBAS FAKHRAVAR: IRAN

Amir Abbas Fakhravar was sentenced to eight years' imprisonment in November 2002, because of comments on Iran's political leadership. In February 2003, he and imprisoned student demonstrator Ahmad Batebi signed an open letter which criticised the Iranian authorities. His cell in the detention centre reportedly had no windows, and was entirely coloured creamy white, as were his clothes. At meal times, he was reportedly given white rice on white, disposable paper plates and if he needed to use the toilet, he had to put a white slip of paper under the door of the cell to alert guards, who reportedly had footwear designed to muffle any sound. He was forbidden to speak to anyone. This technique of sensory deprivation is called 'white torture'. Such conditions of extreme sensory deprivation appear to be designed to weaken the prisoner by causing persistent and unjustified suffering, which amounts to torture.

(Source: adapted from Amnesty International website)

Amnesty International is an organisation that campaigns against such actions and fights to win the release of the prisoners. It brings cases to public notice and encourages ordinary people around the world to write letters of complaint to the governments responsible.

SHI TAO: PEOPLE'S REPUBLIC OF CHINA

In 2005, the Chinese journalist Shi Tao was sentenced to 10 years in prison for sending an email. He had sent an email from his Yahoo! account to a western website reporting that the Chinese government had ordered journalists not to report the fifteenth anniversary of the 1989 crackdown on activists supporting democracy in China.

Activity

1 Read about the cases on this page and find more from websites such as Amnesty International or Reporters Sans Frontières.
2 Write a PowerPoint presentation on prisoners of conscience and deliver it to your class.
3 Write a letter about the treatment of one of the prisoners of conscience you have found out about. In the letter, give reasons why you think journalists should be free to write about problems and difficulties in their home country.

Would you speak out?

Courageous people have dared to speak out when they think something is wrong, even though they have faced imprisonment or intimidation. We like to believe that we live in a free country and that we have the right to say what we think. But do we all use that freedom?

What about you? There are lots of times when you might be called upon to express a view, tell the truth, fight for a cause that you believe in or go against most of your friends. What would you do?

Activity

Work in pairs and decide what you would do in each of the following situations. You can choose: 'Speak out', 'Stay silent' or 'It depends …' (but you'll have to say what it depends on).

1 Tell your employer if a fellow-worker at your weekend job is stealing

4 Stand up for someone who is being bullied by your friends

7 Make a complaint to their company if someone is rude to you or another customer

2 Write a letter to a newspaper supporting a cause that you really feel strongly about

5 Tell someone you know that you don't like them making racist jokes

8 Identify a person who has attacked someone else, if you know who did it

6 Ring the police if someone is behaving suspiciously at a station or on a train

3 Offer to be a witness in a court case if you have seen a crime being committed

9 Defend someone who you think has been treated unjustly at your school

Reflection

How well do you think you're doing?
Think back over the work you have done in Section 3.

Skills

- Draw a chart like the one below, and give yourself a grade from 1 to 5, where 1 is the lowest and 5 is the highest.
- Give evidence for your score and say how you could improve your skills.

Assessing your progress
In this section you will be assessing how well you can:
- examine different sources of information
- debate your views with other people
- develop your campaigning skills
- practise your presentation skills
- think about ways of solving global problems
- develop your understanding of human rights and responsibilities.

How well can you … ?	1	2	3	4	5	Evidence for your score?	How can you improve?
examine different sources of information							
debate your views with other people							
make presentations							
plan campaigns							

Understanding

- Complete the following sentences:
  'Human rights are …'
  'Two key human rights documents are …'
  'We need to protect people's human rights because …'
  'Press freedom is important because …'
- What are the main factors causing so many people to move around the world?
- Which organisation does this logo represent and what work does this organisation do?

- Talk to another pupil and discuss what you think was the most important thing you learned in this section.

Glossary

active citizen someone who wants to change things for the better, who is prepared to argue for and take action to change things or resist an unwanted change

campaign the activities people undertake to persuade people to support their cause

civil liberties the right to freedom of speech and action

community a group of people who live near each other in a local area; a group of people who share common beliefs or ways of life

councillor a person who is elected to sit on a council

court a place where a judge or magistrate tries cases and sentences those found guilty

culture things we learn from our upbringing and the people around us including traditions, beliefs and values that influence our behaviour

democracy a system of government where people regularly elect their leaders and have a say in the way a country is governed

discrimination treating someone unfairly because of your prejudices

election a way of choosing someone for a particular position by voting

fairness treating people in a just, unbiased way

global interdependence the way countries depend on each other, through trade, for their survival and well-being

government the group of people who run a country

human rights rights that are held to belong to any person. The United Nations Universal Declaration of Human Rights, 1948, sets out a full list of the rights that all people should have. These include the right to life, liberty, education, freedom of movement and equality before the law

identity who somebody is; the view people have of themselves which often includes the group(s) to which they belong, such as ethnic or religious group

intolerance refusing to accept that other people have a right to be different; not tolerating other people's views, beliefs and behaviour

justice ensuring that people are treated fairly, without favour to any group, so that everybody can enjoy their rights and freedoms

law a rule that has the backing of the government

legal system the processes and institutions, e.g. courts, that make and uphold our laws

magistrate a member of the local community, with training and legal advice, who deals with cases that are brought before magistrates' and youth courts

migration people moving from place to another to live and work there

offender someone who has broken the law

opinion what somebody thinks about a particular issue; not fact

participation taking part in the life of a school, community or organisation, involving individuals meeting and working with each other

people trafficking when people are tricked or forced to leave their homes and move to another place or country where they are exploited in slave-like work

poverty where a person in a community lacks the essentials for a minimum standard of well-being and life

prejudice opinions that we form without knowing all the facts or much information

press freedom the ability of the press to write what they like

punishment a penalty for a crime or offence: for example, school detention, imprisonment

responsibility recognising what you owe to other people in your community; acting towards other people in a caring or thoughtful way; being accountable for your own actions

rights claims and privileges we expect to have, how we want to be treated by others

rules the code of behaviour that is laid down in a group or organisation, which everyone is expected to obey

sentence the punishment given to a person who has been found guilty in court

services jobs done by the local council for the benefit of people living in the area it controls, e.g. running the library, cleaning the streets

slavery is when people are 'owned' or controlled by an employer; or forced to work by being threatened physically or mentally; or treated as a 'thing' rather than a human being, even being bought and sold; and/or have restrictions placed on their freedom to leave somewhere

stereotype a description of groups of people who have something in common, such as their religion, their age, their sex or their nationality. The description is applied to everyone in the group and ignores individual differences between people

Index